ESTATE PLANNING

FOR THE

Florida Resident

THOMAS N. SILVERMAN, P.A.

**Financial Center at the Gardens
3801 PGA Boulevard, Suite 902
Palm Beach Gardens, Florida 33410
561.775.7500**

WWW.EstatePlanningForTheFloridaResident.COM

Estate Planning for the Florida Resident

Copyright © 2012 by Thomas N. Silverman, Esq.

Previous edition © 1998

Published by

1071 Beechwood Boulevard, LLC

**Attention attorneys, accountants, trust officers, financial planners,
planned giving representatives, life insurance agents and financial
product wholesalers:**
Quantity discounts are available on bulk purchases of this book to be used
as gifts or premiums for your client base or donors. Books personalized
with your name and/or logo and shorter booklets can also be created to fit
specific needs.

Estate Planning is an individual and personal matter for each person and his or her family. Current financial circumstances and long-term financial goals differ, as do relationships between family members and different generations. Tax laws are subject to interpretation and frequent revision. This book is not intended to be a substitute for individual tax and legal advice. No reader should undertake any of the suggestions described in this book without first consulting competent professional advisors.

Cover photographs (small) © iStockphoto.com/Andrea Hill, spxChrome and Troels Graugaard. Cover photograph (large) © Christopher Fay, used under license. Rear cover photograph © iStockphoto.com/DNY59.

Printed in the United States of America.

Library of Congress Catalogue Number: 2001118844

ISBN 9780966429800

ACKNOWLEDGMENTS

No book is solely the product of any one mind. The idea for this book evolved as an outgrowth of an original four (4) page pamphlet written, *circa* 1970, by Ralph C. Richards, Esquire, of the Clearwater, Florida, Bar entitled "What to do with your money when you come to Florida." The author wishes to thank Charles T. Weiss, Esquire, for his valuable contributions to and review of this (fifth) edition of the book. The author also gratefully acknowledges the suggestions and recommendations provided by valued colleagues Richard B. Comiter, Esquire, and Denis Kleinfeld, Esquire and by Samuel B. Silverman, Yale University, Class of 2010.

STATEMENT REQUIRED BY U.S. TREASURY DEPARTMENT: To the extent that this Book contains tax advice, the U.S. Treasury Department requires us to inform you that any advice contained herein is not intended or written by our firm to be used and cannot be used by any taxpayer for the purpose of avoiding any penalties that may be imposed under the Internal Revenue Code. Advice from our firm relating to Federal Tax matters may not be used in promoting, marketing or recommending any entity, investment plan or arrangement to any taxpayer.

ABOUT THE AUTHOR

Thomas N. Silverman, a graduate of the University of Miami and Duquesne Law School, is a member of both the Pennsylvania and Florida Bars and is admitted to practice before the United States Tax Court. He holds a Master of Laws Degree in Taxation from New York University as well as an advanced law degree from Harvard Law School.

Mr. Silverman formerly served as Corporate Counsel to Westinghouse Electric Corporation, and is a past Chairman of the Probate and Guardianship Committee of the 3,000+ member Palm Beach County Bar Association. He is a Florida Bar Board Certified Tax Lawyer and a frequent lecturer on various tax-related subjects, and has written extensively on legal/tax planning concepts and strategies.

Mr. Silverman has practiced law in Palm Beach County, Florida, since 1975, and specializes in Taxation, Estate Planning, Trust and Estate Administration, and related litigation. He is an AV Preeminent Rated Lawyer by Lexis Nexus Martindale-Hubbell.

AUTHOR'S NOTE

No American is under a constitutional duty to pay the highest taxes.

Oliver Wendell Holmes,
United States Supreme Court Justice

In this spirit and in recognition that the tax laws of this country are vast and complex and that our government makes little effort to advise its population, directly, on the existence and changes of such laws, the Author has endeavored to explain the fundamentals of our present transfer tax system; and, in combination with their Florida counterparts, their effects on Floridians who seek to transfer their property to the natural objects of their bounty during their life as gifts or at death as part of their Estates.

This book has been revised, since its original form in 1985, to reflect changes in Federal, State and Local tax laws as well as Internal Revenue Service Statutes, Regulations and Rulings. Every attempt has been made to provide you, the reader, with the most up-to-date information available on this subject. However, this book is not intended to be legal advice, and, as with all educational summaries, the reader should refrain from taking (individual) action without the counsel and guidance of a knowledgeable professional tax advisor.

TABLE OF CONTENTS

LIST OF EXHIBITS

INTRODUCTION

Many current Florida residents formerly resided in other states. The reasons why these people moved to Florida are varied. Some people cite the weather and others espouse the aesthetics of their particular area or the Florida lifestyle. But, whether people come to Florida to retire on the golf course or to stroll in the sun, they find an Estate Planning environment which has been carefully fashioned to fulfill the needs of most of Florida's population. Florida's rapidly expanding economy offers to its younger residents the opportunity to build and augment their Estates. For older residents, there are liberal laws governing Trusts, Estates and Probate administration. Such laws assist with the transfer of assets from one generation to the next, with a minimum of expense, delay and shrinkage from Court costs, taxes and attorney's fees.

Today's mobile lifestyle and multiple home ownership have caused the question of domicile to become more difficult to determine. For example, if a person winters in Florida, spends the spring in Arizona, then moves on to his or her summer home in Cape Cod and, lastly, spends the fall in New York City attending to business affairs, where is his or her state of domicile?

This question becomes even more important when the time comes to levy death taxes. Each state will make its own separate determination regarding the decedent's domicile. If the evidence is ambiguous, this could result in more than one state claiming the decedent as its domiciliary, with each seeking to impose its own Inheritance Tax on the decedent's entire Estate.

Under Florida Law, for purposes of Estate Taxes, an individual is *presumed* to have died domiciled in Florida if he or she dwelt in the state for any period of twelve (12) consecutive months in the twenty-four (24) months preceding death, notwithstanding whether such person may have traveled outside the state, voted in Florida or was assessed taxes in the State of Florida.

Generally, there are two (2) occasions which prompt an inquiry or investigation by a foreign jurisdiction when a person changes his or her domicile to Florida.

First, a new resident can expect follow-up questions from a former state of domicile when he or she stops filing State Income Tax returns there. The fact that such a last filing is a "final return" should be denoted on the return itself, if such is true.

Accompanying the return should be a copy of the person's Declaration of Non-Domicile filed with his/or her former state of residency and/or a copy of his or her Declaration of Domicile filed in Florida. See Exhibits I, II and III of this book for examples.

Second, if a new resident continues to retain significant contacts with his or her former state, which are of a type that could create doubts as to his or her legal domicile, then it is wise to avoid matters which are likely to come to the attention of the taxing authorities of the former state.

Ownership of real estate in the state of former domicile creates the greatest danger. Real estate is a form of property which attracts special attention in various ways including the County Court Clerk who records transfers and potential purchasers, title insurance companies, banks and mortgage companies in the process of checking titles, liens, real property records, taxes, etc.

Furthermore, an Estate Tax is often payable to the former state on the value of real property owned by the decedent and located within that jurisdiction. This is true regardless of whether a Florida domicile has been validly established. And, during the review period following the decedent's death, the tax department of the former state may decide to claim that the decedent's entire Estate is taxable there.

Consider, for example, a person who owns a home in his/or her former state of domicile, where he or she continues to stay for five (5) months of the year, and where he or she retains affiliations with his or her old church or synagogue, country club, bank and other contacts. These circumstances could cause a serious Estate Tax problem. This client would be well advised to consider transferring ownership of the real estate to another family member or perhaps to a family Trust, partnership, corporation or limited liability company, or to make another similar satisfactory disposition of the property. Then, upon death, there is no transfer of title to such real estate which would prompt an inquiry into the real estate ownership, and the former state's tax department is less likely to become involved.

There are several Estate Planning steps that can be taken to clarify the domicile question and which are recommended for persons changing their domicile to Florida. Some of these factors are set forth as follows:

1. File a Declaration of Non-Domicile with the state and county of former residence. Established procedures may be absent and improvisation required. (See Exhibit I)

2. File a Florida Declaration of Domicile in the Office of the Clerk of the Circuit Court in the Florida county in which you reside. (See Exhibit II) If a residence is also maintained in another state, a Special Declaration of Domicile should be filed. (See Exhibit III)

3. Declare in your Will that you are a legal resident of the State of Florida, and execute all Estate Planning documents in Florida.

4. Transfer bank accounts, safe deposit boxes and securities to Florida institutions (safe deposit boxes in Florida are not sealed upon death of a lessee or a co-lessee).

5. Register to vote in Florida and actually vote in all elections.

6. Register your boat and/or automobile in Florida, and obtain a Florida Driver License. If a non-driver, obtain a Florida Identification Card.

7. Discard your out-of-state driver's license.

8. File your Federal Income Tax return with the District Director of Internal Revenue Service where prescribed for filing by Florida residents.

9. State that you are a resident of Florida, and use your Florida address in all business transactions.

10. Change social, religious and other national organization memberships to Florida affiliations or branches, and use your Florida address in all correspondence and/or membership data.

11. Own a home or lease an apartment in Florida, move in, and furnish this home or apartment more extensively than any other residence.

12. When traveling out of Florida, register as being from Florida, and give a Florida address or post office box.

13. Obtain a Library Card from the local (Florida) City, or County Public Library.

14. File non-resident State Income Tax returns in the state of former residence if you continue to have local income from sources within that state.

15. Change advisors, such as banker, accountant, lawyer, account executive, financial planner and/or life insurance professional, to those located in Florida rather than in the northern state.

16. Relinquish the return trip portion of any round-trip airline tickets to destinations in your former state of residence.

17. Refrain from referring to any northern residence as your "home" in Estate Planning documents.

18. Reduce charitable contributions to northern organizations in favor of increased donations to Florida charitable entities.

19. Relinquish telephone number listings and all other utility billings in your name in your former state of residence.

20. Apply for Florida Homestead Exemption, if qualified.

21. Keep stays in nursing/retirement homes in other states to a minimum and only if authorized or required by a Florida physician.

22. Move art objects, jewelry, antiques and all other substantial items of personal property to your Florida residence.

23. Consider maintaining a personal log or journal evidencing days spent in Florida, and elsewhere, to validate claims of Florida domicile.

24. Transact business in Florida and render services, where possible, in Florida under written documents requiring same.

25. Do not claim residency in a state other than Florida to receive discounts for goods and/or services.

The timing of any change of domicile to Florida is important, especially for Income Tax purposes in the state of former residence. For example, by establishing Florida domicile prior to January 1st, you will avoid the requirement of filing a resident State Income Tax return in your former state for the upcoming year. And, in some instances, you may be able to avoid State Income Tax on sales of homes and/or businesses by precise timing of your change in domicile to Florida from your former state of residence.

In instances of disputed domicile at death, the State of Florida has enacted a Statute which authorizes the Florida Department of Revenue to litigate, on behalf of the Florida Estate of a deceased person, the question of determination of domicile for Inheritance Tax purposes.

As favorable taxes are often mentioned by persons considering a change of their domicile to Florida, before turning our attention to a discussion of specific Florida Tax Laws, it may be helpful to consider what types of taxes the State of Florida does *not* impose upon its residents.

Tax Advantages to Florida Domicile

No State Income Tax. The State of Florida does not have a personal Income Tax. A prohibition against such a tax was originally drafted into Florida's Constitution in 1885. This prohibition was re-enacted in the 1968 Constitution and remains a part of Florida's present Constitution. In order to enact a personal Income Tax, Florida's Constitution would have to be amended. Such an action would require approval by vote of the citizens of the State of Florida.

No City Income Tax. Although various cities (such as those in the northeast) impose Local Income Taxes of their own, Florida municipalities are prohibited from doing so.

No Florida Gift Tax. Residents of a number of states (e.g., Connecticut, Tennessee, North Carolina and Louisiana) may pay state as well as Federal Tax on gifts made during their lifetimes. Florida residents pay no State Gift Tax.

No State Death Tax. Florida does not have a State Death Tax, and the credit for State Death Taxes it previously received has been abolished.

In contrast to the Florida Estate Tax Law, some states (e.g., Connecticut, Tennessee, Ohio and Pennsylvania) impose a separate tax on a **beneficiary's** right to inherit or receive property. This is sometimes known as an Inheritance Tax and results in the heirs or beneficiaries paying taxes twice, although a deduction for the State Inheritance Tax is allowed in computing the (total) Taxable Estate that will be subject to Federal Estate Taxes. (See Exhibit IV)

For those non-residents who die owning taxable property in Florida, the tax imposed is not unlike that imposed upon the Estate of a Florida resident. Taxable property of a non-resident decedent includes: Florida real property, tangible personal property having an actual situs in Florida, intangible personal property having a business situs in Florida, and securities of a Florida corporation.

When a Florida resident owns property (especially real property) physically located in another state, the use of a Florida partnership, Revocable (Living) Trust, Personal Residence Trust, limited liability company or closely-held Florida corporation to hold such property may avoid such property becoming subject to a State Death Tax and/or Inheritance Tax in that other state, which, as mentioned, would be **in addition to** the Federal Estate Tax.

Florida Real Estate Tax

In Florida, real estate taxes are assessed as of January 1st of each year, but are not payable until the following November 1st. Taxes are assessed on a calendar year basis. Thus, real estate taxes for any year become a technical lien against the real property as of January 1st of that year, but are not payable until the 1st of November when the tax bills are issued. Taxes for any year become delinquent if not paid by April 1st of the succeeding year.

The State of Florida imposes no tax on real estate, but such tax is usually imposed by the county and by the municipality in which the property is located.

Each county has a property appraiser and a tax collector. In previous years, municipalities also had their own tax officials which frequently resulted in confusion on the part of the taxpayer. The Florida Legislature resolved the matter by passing legislation which allows each county appraiser to assess and collect real estate taxes for individual cities as well as for the county. As a result, county taxes and city taxes are now included in one bill, sent by the County Tax Collector.

Florida Real Estate Homestead Tax Exemption. In 1934, to assist its residents in their struggle against the hard economic times brought about by the Great Depression, Florida amended its

Constitution to provide that the Homesteads of its citizens would be exempt from taxation up to a value of five thousand dollars ($5,000). This means that Homesteads having a value of five thousand dollars ($5,000) or less paid no real property taxes at all. Other Homesteads paid tax only on the assessed value in excess of five thousand dollars ($5,000).

Although the original purpose for the Homestead Exemption has long since disappeared, this particular tax benefit afforded to Florida residents has been expanded and increased. Since 1983, a twenty-five thousand dollars ($25,000) Exemption has been afforded to all homeowners who are domiciled in Florida as of January 1st of a particular year. (There is no longer a five-year residency requirement for obtaining a full Homestead Tax Exemption.) Additional recent amendments to the Florida Homestead Law provided that the benefits of Homestead Tax Exemption extend to persons occupying property under a contract to purchase if the contract is duly recorded; that a surviving spouse who occupies the Homestead following the death of their spouse may claim the Homestead Tax Exemption; extended the Homestead Tax Exemption to owners of cooperative apartments and those condominium apartment projects built upon land owned in fee by the condominium as well as those projects built upon leaseholds, provided the leasehold has an original term of ninety-eight (98) years or more (an important consideration for those people who plan to buy a condominium apartment in Florida); and provided for continued entitlement to the Homestead Tax Exemption to those individuals who transfer title of their "Homestead" property to a Revocable Trust or Declaration of Trust, in which the transferee enjoys the right to the use and occupancy of the property for their lifetime.

Since 1995, Florida homeowners have also been afforded a three percent (3%) cap on increases in the assessed value of Homestead through the Save Our Homes Constitutional amendment.

Under a new Constitutional amendment passed by Florida voters on January 29, 2008, the Florida Homestead Exemption increased from twenty-five thousand dollars ($25,000) to fifty thousand dollars ($50,000) on a Homestead having an assessed value of greater than seventy-five thousand dollars ($75,000). No additional application for the increased Exemption is necessary if the homeowner was already receiving the prior twenty-five thousand dollar ($25,000) Exemption. Under the same legislation, homeowners currently receiving Exemption benefits may sell their current Homestead and transfer a portion of the accumulated Save Our Homes tax savings to a new Homestead that also qualifies for Homestead Exemption benefits. If the new Homestead has a higher assessed value than the prior Homestead, the homeowner is entitled to transfer the amount of the accumulated savings to the new home, up to five hundred thousand dollars ($500,000), thereby lowering the assessed value by the same amount. For example, if the prior Homestead has a just value of five hundred thousand dollars ($500,000), but because of Save Our Homes, the assessed value is only two hundred thousand dollars ($200,000), the difference of three hundred thousand dollars ($300,000) may be applied to reduce the assessed value, of the new Homestead. The amount of the accumulated savings that is eligible for transfer will be a percentage of the tax savings. Using the example above, the ratio of the assessed value to the just value ($200,000 / $500,000 = $40%) is the amount that may be applied to the assessed value of the new Homestead (40% x $300,000 = $120,000).

Florida Tangible Personal Property Tax. The Florida Legislature has exempted from taxation all household furnishings, wearing apparel, effects of the person actually employed in the use of serving the creature comforts of the owner and *not held* for commercial purposes. Now, a person may own household goods of any value to serve his or her "creature comforts," and these goods will not be subject to taxation.

However, any tangible personal property used for the production of income, such as furniture and furnishings in an office or rental apartment, is taxable. A tax return covering such items must be filed no later than April 1st of each year, and a ten percent (10%) penalty is assessed for failure to file the return.

Motor vehicles, boats, trailers, trailer coaches and mobile homes are subject to an annual license tax but are not subject to ad valorem taxation.

Note: Mobile homes without a current license plate *are* subject to tangible personal property tax, while a mobile home permanently affixed to the land on which it is located is presumed to be real estate if the land is also owned by the mobile home owner.

Florida Intangible Personal Property Tax. The State of Florida previously imposed a tax on the intangible personal property of every person who was a legal resident of Florida as of January 1st of every year. "Intangible" property is that which has no value of itself, but represents something of value. For example, stocks, bonds, notes and other accounts receivable were subject to the tax. However, specifically excluded from the tax was money (including cash and certificates of deposit), copyrights and patents, and certain Federal, State and Local government bonds, as well as other items. The Florida Intangible Personal Property Tax was abolished for all years after 2006.

Florida has made a special effort to encourage people to relocate here in the latter stages of life by enacting a series of favorable Estate, Trust and Tax laws which allow its residents to pass on as much of their property as possible to heirs and/or family members with a minimum amount of cost and delay.

Much can be accomplished through the use of self-Declarations of Trust, self-proving wills and joint tenancies with right of survivorship. Safe deposit boxes are not sealed in Florida at the death of a joint tenant because Florida has no State Inheritance Tax. Florida recognizes spendthrift trust provisions which protect trust beneficiaries from the claims of creditors. Also, Florida has enacted laws which (i) treat inherited or gifted property as "non-marital assets" in divorce proceedings and (ii) protect retirement plan benefits from claims of creditors. As Florida's population has increased, the number of "second" marriages which occur in the state has also increased, making more important the resolution of legal issues which inevitably arise with multiple marriages and "second" family situations.

In the pages that follow, the laws of Florida which relate to these important subjects have been reduced to their most understandable terms to give the reader a working knowledge of their essential elements.

It is quite possible that the Will of a current Florida resident was executed in another state. Therefore, the question arises as to whether such Will is valid under Florida Law. Generally, a Will is valid in Florida if it was valid in the state in which it was executed, except for Wills handwritten by the Testator and not attested to by two (2) witnesses. However, there are overriding considerations for having a "Florida" Will.

Witnesses to an out-of-state Will may be extremely difficult to locate following the Testator's death. It may also be inconvenient to have prior witnesses acknowledge or give testimony in order to "prove" the Will. As the Courts require that the Personal Representative or attorney perform a diligent search to locate a witness to the Will, this would involve additional expense in the Probate of the Testator's Estate.

Under Florida's Probate Code, a Florida Will may now be executed before a Notary Public, who acknowledges that the Testator signed the Will before the two (2) witnesses, who themselves acknowledge the Testator's signature and that the Testator was competent at the time of execution of the Will. If the Will is "self-proved," that is, executed before a Notary Public with the foregoing requirements, the Will may be automatically admitted to Probate in Florida without the requirement of locating a witness to obtain his or her Oath as a witness to the Will. However, while the law does not require the witnesses or Notary Public to be uninterested parties (those who do not stand to inherit from the Estate), such laws could change, and the better practice is to have unrelated and uninterested parties act as witnesses and Notary to the execution of a Will. This will lessen the possibility of a Will contest by a disgruntled heir seeking to have the Will set aside.

The Will should recite the person's place of domicile at the time of execution. Accordingly, if the Testator has recently become a resident of Florida, his or her Will can act as additional proof of his or her change of domicile. As previously stated, it is not uncommon to have two (2) states claim that a decedent was domiciled in both for tax purposes. This is especially true where an individual continues to return to his or her former state of domicile during the summer months or continues to own real property or other significant assets located in the other state. The recital as to domicile should refer only to the State of Florida.

In Florida, the position formerly known as executor or executrix and administrator or administratrix, is now referred to as the Personal Representative of the Estate. Under Florida Law, the Personal Representative of the Estate must be either a Florida resident or related to the Testator to a certain degree.

In addition, even though a Will may contain provisions waiving the furnishing of a bond to ensure the faithful performance of the duties of the Personal Representative, it is possible, especially if the Will was not executed in Florida, that the Probate Court will require the Personal Representative to post a surety bond. This can mean additional expense and inconvenience for the Personal Representative and delay the Probate proceeding.

The terms of a Will can also be used to waive certain duties imposed on Personal Representatives under Florida Law. For example, the Testator may wish to waive the requirement of furnishing bond or the filing of periodic Accountings in the Estate or may wish to authorize the Personal Representative to sell real property without Court approval. Waiver of these requirements, if honored by the Probate Court, can save time and money in the Probate administration.

Finally, there are circumstances which compel a review of an existing Estate Plan, including the making of a new Will or Codicil to an old Will. For example, a change of residence (e.g., from New York to Florida), change in financial resources, retirement, divorce or remarriage, and the birth of children or grandchildren are significant changes in circumstances. A Will should be revised whenever a significant change in circumstances occurs so that it will conform to the person's needs and desires. In light of the recent and continuing changes in the tax laws, including the Economic Growth and Tax Relief Reconciliation

Act of 2001, almost every Will signed before 1986 should be reviewed and updated.

Codicil(s). A Codicil is a change to a Last Will and Testament. It may only be made by a writing signed with the same formalities as the original Will. Since 1976, all Wills and Codicils require execution before **at least** two (2) witnesses and a Notary Public to be self-proved. No alterations of a Will should be made on the face of the Instrument. To do so may jeopardize the validity and effectiveness of the entire Will and, perhaps, cause the Testator's Estate to pass by intestacy (i.e., without a Will). The assistance of a qualified attorney is recommended in this area.

Oral Will(s). Oral Wills are not valid in Florida under any circumstances whatsoever.

REQUIREMENTS OF A VALID FLORIDA WILL

1. The Testator must be at least eighteen (18) years old.

2. The Testator must be of sound mind, i.e., able to understand the extent of his or her property, the natural objects of his or her bounty and the nature of his or her disposition.

3. The Testator must be free from fraud and undue influence.

4. The Will must be signed by the Testator or by someone else for him or her in his or her presence and at his or her direction. Such signature can be a mark or symbol if affixed with the intent that it constitute a signature.

5. The Will must be signed at the end of the document. Signing, or acknowledgment thereof, must be in the presence of at least two (2) witnesses who must attest to the Will in the presence of the Testator and in the presence of each other. Note that the witnesses need not see the Testator sign as long as the Testator acknowledges his or her signature in their presence. Although it is not recommended, interested persons can serve as witnesses without jeopardizing their interests under the Will.

The use of a "self-proving" affidavit avoids the necessity of searching for witnesses after the Testator's death to prove the Will by their testimony. Such an affidavit, signed by the Testator and by both witnesses, may be executed at the time of, or subsequent to, execution of the Will.

The Custodian (holder) of the original Will must deposit such Will with the court within ten (10) days after learning of the Testator's death. Willful failure to do so without reasonable cause makes the Custodian liable for any costs and damages sustained.

Recording of a Will in the public records prior to death is not a legal requirement to its validity and has no legal effect in Florida (except making such Will a part of the public records).

Appointment of a Personal Representative

One of the most important functions of a Will is the appointment of a Personal Representative of the Testator's Estate. The Personal Representative is responsible for gathering the Decedent's assets, paying valid debts of the Decedent and expenses of administering the Estate (including taxes), and finally, making distributions to beneficiaries. The office of Personal Representative is an important one, and the choice for the Personal Representative and the successor should be given serious consideration.

Generally, a person who is a Florida resident, at least eighteen (18) years of age, of sound mind, and not previously convicted of a felony, may serve as a Personal Representative. A nonresident of Florida may only serve as Personal Representative if he or she is related to the Decedent in one of the following ways: legally adopted child or adoptive parent; lineal ascendant (grandparent) or descendant (child or grandchild); spouse, brother, sister, aunt, uncle, nephew or niece; a lineal ascendant or descendant of any such person; or a spouse of any such person. A blood relative of a deceased spouse will not qualify to serve as Personal Representative of a Florida Estate.

Also, any trust company incorporated under the laws of the State of Florida and authorized to exercise fiduciary powers in the State may act as a Personal Representative.

Note: An individual's selection of another in their Will to serve as Personal Representative may not be honored by a Probate Judge if such named individual exhibits bad behavior, is conflicted, or acts in a manner which is not in the best interest of the decedent's Estate. In other words, the Probate Court has discretion to refuse to appoint a designated individual who is demonstrated to be unfit to serve due to lack of character, integrity or the like.

Guardian of Minor Children

A Will may be used to appoint a Guardian for a minor child in the event of the deaths of both parents of a minor child. In the absence of a Will or the appointment of a Guardian in a Will, or a Declaration Naming Pre-Need Guardian for Minor (which is attached as Exhibit XII to this book), Florida Law controls who will be appointed as Guardian of a deceased parent's minor children. A Declaration of Pre-Need Guardian (similar to that appearing as Exhibit XII) may also be used to name a Guardian for an adult individual's person and/or property in the event of their incapacity.

INTESTATE SUCCESSION UNDER FLORIDA LAW

Distribution of the Intestate Estate

When a person dies without a valid Will or other Testamentary Instrument in Florida, that person is deemed to have died *Intestate.* In such event, the laws of Intestate Succession in Florida set forth the disposition of all property separately owned by the decedent based upon whether the decedent was married at the time of death and whether the decedent left any surviving lineal descendants (such as children or grandchildren) or, in the alternative, other surviving heirs of the decedent. For example, if a decedent died with a surviving spouse but no surviving lineal descendants, the surviving spouse would inherit all of the decedent's Intestate Estate. In addition, the surviving spouse would inherit all of the decedent's Intestate Estate if the decedent is survived by one or more descendants, all of whom are also descendants of the surviving spouse, and the surviving spouse has no other descendant.

However, if any of the decedent's lineal descendants are not also lineal descendants of the surviving spouse, or if the surviving spouse has other descendants who are not lineal descendants of the decedent, then the surviving spouse would inherit one-half (½) of the decedent's Intestate property and lineal descendants would share the other one-half (½).

In the event the decedent did not leave a surviving spouse, but did have lineal descendants surviving at his or her death, then all Intestate property would pass to the decedent's lineal descendants, again on an equal basis.

If the decedent did not have any lineal descendants or surviving spouse, then all Intestate property would pass, first, to the decedent's parents, if living; otherwise, to the decedent's surviving brothers and sisters. There are further provisions under the Florida Law of Intestacy for distribution to more remote relatives if none of the foregoing is living at the time of the decedent's death. And, if the decedent leaves no ascertainable relatives, his or her entire Estate passes to the State of Florida School Fund by *escheat.*

The laws of Intestate Succession also apply to determine who inherits property not effectively distributed under a valid Last Will and Testament. For example, Mr. Smith dies owning two properties: Blackacre and Whiteacre. At his death, Mr. Smith leaves a valid Will which specifically bequeaths Blackacre to a named beneficiary. Mr. Smith is considered to have died Intestate *as to Whiteacre*, and the Laws of Intestacy govern who inherits that property.

Appointment of Personal Representative of an Intestate Estate

When a person dies without a valid Will, the Probate Court determines who shall serve as Personal Representative of the decedent's Estate. Preference is given to the surviving spouse, then to the person selected by a majority in interest of the heirs, and then to the heir nearest in relation to the decedent, with the Probate Court deciding who shall serve if more than one heir of the same relation to the decedent requests appointment. The Probate Court also has the authority to (and often does) require the Personal Representative of an Intestate Estate to post a surety bond, which can be a substantial expense to the Estate. This requirement may be waived in a valid Last Will and Testament, but such provision is no guarantee that the Probate Court will not require a bond.

Guardianship of Intestate Decedent's Minor/Incapacitated Children

In the case of a minor or incapacitated child in Intestacy situations, the Probate Court designates a formal Guardian for the person and property of such child, which may or may not be someone whom the decedent would have approved. This can also be avoided by a parent designating a Guardian in his or her valid Last Will and Testament or in a Declaration Naming Pre-Need Guardian for Minor.

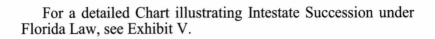

For a detailed Chart illustrating Intestate Succession under Florida Law, see Exhibit V.

PRETERMITTED CHILDREN — RIGHTS OF CHILDREN BORN OR ADOPTED AFTER THE MAKING OF A WILL

When a Testator fails to provide in a Will for any child born or adopted after the making of the Will, and such child has not received an advancement of the Testator's property equivalent to a child's part (unless it appears from the Will that such omission was intentional, or unless the Testator had one or more children when the Will was executed and devised substantially all of his or her Estate to the other parent of the pretermitted child), such child shall receive a share in the Estate of the Testator equal in value to that which he would have received if the Testator had died Intestate. Note that under Florida Law, children living at the time of the making of the Will are not protected and, in fact, can be intentionally or accidentally disinherited.

PRETERMITTED SPOUSE —
THE EFFECT OF A SUBSEQUENT MARRIAGE ON A PRIOR WILL

When a person marries after making a Will, and is survived by his or her spouse, such a surviving spouse is entitled to a share in the deceased spouse's Estate equal in value to that which such surviving spouse would have received had the Testator died Intestate. Thus, such spouse is characterized as a "Pretermitted Spouse." The above rule will not apply if (i) provision has been made for or waived by the surviving spouse in a marriage contract or in the Will; or (ii) the Testator of the Will discloses an intention not to make a provision for the surviving spouse. The Elective Share of a surviving spouse, as discussed later, is not defeated by the pretermitted spouse rule and continues to be exercisable. Generally, however, the Intestate share for a surviving spouse will exceed by percentage the amount of the Elective Share, so, for practical purposes, the right of election may seldom be exercised by a Pretermitted Spouse.

Please note that recent changes in Florida Law relating to the Elective Share of a spouse, which became effective for all decedents dying after October 1, 2001, extend the base or nature of property subject to the Elective Share to Revocable Trust assets, In-Trust-For (ITF) bank accounts, jointly-owned property and life insurance, among other classes of property, while the Intestate share of a surviving spouse in their deceased spouse's Estate is based only upon property which is subject to administration, i.e., property owned by the decedent in his or her own name.

The term "Probate" refers to the legal process of transferring legal title of assets owned by an individual *in his or her individual name* at death to his or her intended beneficiaries under a valid Last Will and Testament, or to his or her heirs if no Will exists.

There are two ways in the State of Florida to transfer property at death: by *operation of law* and by the *Probate* process.

Operation of Law

The most common method for transferring property at death is by *operation of law*, which means that the survivor or intended beneficiary receives the property directly (without passing through the Probate process). This can be accomplished by several different procedures:

Tenancy by the Entireties. This method of transfer is done by spouses taking title to property in their joint names which indicates their marital status and which requires that ownership pass to the surviving spouse upon the death of the other spouse (i.e., right of survivorship). This type of tenancy is automatically created when married persons take title to real property which is to be their principal residence in Florida. This form of joint ownership may only be taken between spouses.

Joint Tenants with Right of Survivorship. This method of transfer is usually undertaken between a parent and child. The controlling document must indicate that title is being taken as "joint tenants with rights of survivorship" (JTWROS), meaning that the survivor of the named individuals will take sole ownership of the property at the death of the first to die. Failure to designate the rights of survivorship will result in the creation of a tenancy-in-common with the decedent's interest in the property passing through the decedent's Estate, and being subject to Probate Administration.

Totten Trusts. This method of transfer is usually utilized with certificates of deposit or accounts at savings or banking institutions. Some brokerage firms also permit accounts to be opened in this manner. As long as the original owner is living, the person for whom the trust is "for the benefit of" has no ownership rights in the property. For example, if a parent opens a savings account at a local bank in his/her own name "in trust for" (ITF) his/her child, the child has no rights to any of those funds until the parent's death. At the parent's death, the child becomes sole owner of the remaining balance of the savings account. This is unlike a joint account where each individual has the current right to withdraw all the funds in the account without the signature of the other party. If, instead, a parent opened a joint account with his/her child, the child would have the right to withdraw all of the money in the account at any time without the parent's permission (assuming the child has reached the age of majority). It is the existence of rights in both the parent and child during the parent's lifetime that distinguishes joint ownership from assets titled "in trust for" another.

Life Insurance Policies. By placing an individual's name on the beneficiary designation portion of a life insurance policy, the insured or owner of the policy provides by contract that the insurance company will distribute the proceeds of the policy to the named beneficiary (other than the Personal Representative of the insured's Estate) upon proof of the insured's death, without the necessity of any Probate proceeding.

Gifts to Minors. By opening accounts or purchasing securities in trust for a minor, a parent or grandparent may nominate a Custodian to hold property for the benefit of a minor. When such minor attains the age of twenty-one (21), the property becomes the minor's property, to do with as he or she desires. In the event the Custodian dies prior to the minor's attaining the age of twenty-one (21), a successor Custodian is named to control the account until the minor's twenty-first (21st) birthday. Since a completed gift of the property is made to the minor, subject to retention until the minor attains the age of twenty-one (21), such property avoids Probate.

Revocable Trusts. Assets transferred to a Revocable Trust or Declaration of Trust during a person's lifetime will avoid Probate at death if the Trust is properly drafted and the assets properly transferred to it during lifetime. Often, assets are improperly transferred to a Revocable Trust or Declaration of Trust, thereby resulting in an unnecessary Probate.

Transfers by Probate

The second manner in which a decedent's property is transferred at death is through the *Probate* process. Property owned solely in the decedent's **individual name** at death must pass through Probate. The Personal Representative has the responsibility of collecting the assets of the decedent, making sure they are all valued and accounted for, paying all creditors' claims (including taxes), and then distributing them to the decedent's beneficiaries if he or she left a valid Last Will and Testament or, in the absence of such, to the decedent's heirs-at-law determined under the laws of Intestate Succession of the State of Florida.

Advantages of Probate. Probate affords flexibility as to the Income Tax Liability of beneficiaries. For Income Tax purposes, certain expenses are deductible by the Estate if incurred by the Personal Representative and passed on to the heirs, and not deductible if there is no Probate and the beneficiaries are obligated to incur the obligations themselves. For larger Estates, major tax savings can be achieved through Probate and the exercise of the choice of beneficial tax years and post-mortem Estate Planning options.

The Probate process offers continuing supervision through the filing of Inventories, Accountings and Notices to Beneficiaries. The Probate Judge can arbitrate disputes that may arise between heirs and beneficiaries.

Probate provides a procedure to identify the decedent's debts, and either pay them or contest them. This is accomplished through a publication of Notice to Creditors (formerly Notice of Administration) in a local newspaper, as well as sending such Notice directly to reasonably ascertainable creditors of the decedent. Following the publication and mailing of such Notices, creditors have a limited amount of time within which to file their claims against the Estate. If a creditor fails to file its claim within the prescribed period of time, it generally may not thereafter file such claim. The Personal Representative may then file an Objection to and contest the claim, pay the claim, or attempt to settle the claim for some lesser amount. This procedure enables the beneficiaries to receive their shares of the Estate free of claims of creditors, and be reasonably certain that no further claims may be asserted.

Lastly, property distributed from a decedent's Probate Estate receives a "step-up" in cost basis when received by the intestate heir or testate beneficiary under a Will. For example, if the decedent paid five thousand dollars ($5,000) for a vacant lot and died years later when the lot was worth one hundred thousand dollars ($100,000), the intestate heirs or testate beneficiaries under a Will would inherit the property with a one hundred thousand dollar ($100,000) basis for future Federal Income Tax purposes.

Disadvantages of Probate. The primary disadvantages to Probate are the attorney's fees, court costs and delays associated with same. If all of a decedent's property is held jointly or passes by operation of law, there is no Probate and, therefore, no additional costs are incurred.

Probate often causes unnecessary delays, whereas the beneficiaries receive non-Probate property (i.e., life insurance, jointly-held property) immediately upon the decedent's death. If the filing of a Federal Estate Tax Return is required, it may take up to three (3) years before a Closing Letter is received from the Internal Revenue Service, entitling the Personal Representative to formally close the Probate proceeding.

It should be noted that the requirements for Probate Administration and the filing of Federal Estate Tax Return are separate, and either or both may be required, depending upon the nature and value of the Estate.

Avoiding Probate. There are many reasons for residents and non-residents to avoid the Probate of their Estates in both foreign and local jurisdictions. The most important reason for avoiding Probate is the duplication of costs incurred in probating the Estate in the state of domicile and in the ancillary (i.e., foreign) state. As a result, many non-residents have elected to take title to Florida property in such a manner as to avoid Ancillary Probate Administration.

The most common methods of Probate avoidance are joint ownership with rights of survivorship and the use of Revocable Trusts. The first method is certainly the simplest and probably the more widely used. However, although joint ownership avoids Probate of the assets at the death of the first owner, it does not avoid Probate upon the death of the surviving joint owner, and, depending upon the size of the Estate, owning property jointly may cause or create unnecessary or additional Estate Taxes upon the passing of the surviving joint-owner. This is due to the possible wasting of the available Unified Credit of the first person to die.

The use of a Trust to hold title to Florida real estate completely avoids the need for ancillary administration by any of the owners of the property. Florida Law provides for use of a Land Trust to hold title to a non-resident's real property. This Trust can provide that all decisions respecting the property be made by the beneficiary rather than the Trustee. The beneficiary can be responsible for payment of taxes, mortgages and other fees. The documents can provide for the succession of the beneficial interest in the property upon the death of a beneficiary. The interest possessed by the beneficiary is considered to be an interest in personalty rather than real property, and, as such, the Trust and the assets of the Trust will not be subject to ancillary Probate administration in Florida upon the death of such beneficiary.

As previously stated, for Florida residents, the creation of (self-controlled) validly formed and operated separate entities to take title to the out-of-state real property can also completely avoid Ancillary Probate and possibly non-resident Estate and/or

Inheritance Taxation in the state where the property is physically located.

Moreover, the use of either a Florida General or Limited Partnership to own non-Florida real property will work equally well in avoiding ancillary Probate and Inheritance Tax, assuming that (1) the owner of the property wishes to take on partners, and (2) the interest in a partnership which owns real property is considered an interest in personalty under the law of the foreign jurisdiction. A Florida corporation or limited liability company could also be used to accomplish the same objectives.

ADVANTAGES AND DISADVANTAGES OF JOINTLY-HELD PROPERTY

Advantages of Joint Ownership

As discussed previously, jointly owned property avoids the necessity of Probate, and passes directly to the surviving joint owner. This "automatic" transfer of property, without Probate, may be helpful to provide a surviving spouse with funds to be used for his or her support if Probate Administration is required for the decedent's other assets. In addition, spouses may own assets as Tenants by Entirety which has creditor protection advantages.

It is also advisable in Florida to have both spouses' names, or the names of two individuals, on a safe deposit box so that there will be access to the box at the time of one party's death, as the State of Florida does not have a separate State Inheritance Tax which would require the sealing of the box at the death of a co-owner.

In the event there is no obligation to file a Federal Estate Tax Return, the holding of jointly-held property can avoid unnecessary Probate costs and transfer all of the assets upon the decedent's death to the survivor. The Personal Representative will merely be required to file an Affidavit obtained from the Department of Revenue of the State of Florida with the Clerk of the Court which is admissible as evidence of non-liability for Florida Estate Tax, and will remove the Florida Department of Revenue lien, thus, clearing title to any real property.

Disadvantages of Joint Ownership

In the event the Estate is required to file a Federal Estate Tax Return, all jointly-held property must be reported on such return. Under prior law, jointly-held property had to be reported at its full fair market value unless the surviving joint owner could prove that he or she contributed to the acquisition of such property. Current law provides that only one-half (½) of the value of the property held jointly with the surviving spouse need be reported on the deceased spouse's Federal Estate Tax Return. Nonetheless, once such asset is reported on the return, it becomes a matter of public record, and upon the death of the surviving spouse, the Internal Revenue Service may look to see if that asset is reported on the surviving spouse's Estate Tax Return at full value, and, if not, may inquire into the present status of such asset.

Many brokerage houses will not transfer or place stock certificates into the surviving joint owner's name until it has been shown that the Federal Estate Taxes have been paid on the property. Therefore, while the surviving joint tenant inherits property outright upon the decedent's death, he or she may not be able to dispose of such property until Closing Letters have been issued by the Internal Revenue Service and the Florida Department of Revenue.

Any property which is held jointly with another person (with the right of survivorship) cannot be devised in the Will of one of the joint owners to a third party, because such property passes outside the Will (i.e., by operation of law). The form of ownership controls the manner in which it passes, as opposed to a Will performing this function. Accordingly, joint ownership lessens the flexibility for dealing with the property, and restricts the owner's testamentary options.

By placing another person's name on the title to certain property, the owner transfers outright ownership to a portion of the property. The placing of a child's name on the title to the owner's condominium or house may result in a completed gift of an interest in that property, requiring the filing of a United States Gift Tax Return and possible payment of Federal and/or State Gift Taxes. The property may not later be sold or otherwise disposed of without the co-owner's permission and signature on all closing papers. Where such co-owner is a minor, a Guardian may be required to be appointed by the Court in order to consent to such a transfer.

Further, the holding of all of an individual's property jointly with his or her spouse will waste the Unified Credit available against Federal Estate Taxes for the first spouse to die, and will often give the government more in taxes than necessary. The tax consequences of such ownership will be discussed further in the pages that follow.

THE REVOCABLE (LIVING) TRUST

The Revocable Trust, or "Living Trust," is established by an individual during his or her lifetime. The Creator of a Revocable Trust is called the "Settlor," and this type of Trust is established primarily for his or her benefit. The Settlor may retain the power to revoke, amend, modify or change the terms of the Trust at any time. The Settlor may also reserve the right to receive the income from the Trust during his or her lifetime as well as retain unrestricted access to the corpus, or principal, of the Trust. Upon the death or permanent incapacity of the Settlor, the Trust becomes irrevocable and may not be subsequently amended.

In drafting a Florida Revocable Trust, the attorney generally utilizes one of two different formats, depending upon the particular circumstances of the Settlor. The conventional Revocable Trust is an agreement between two parties (the Settlor and a separate Trustee), while the Declaration of Trust is a one-party arrangement wherein the Settlor also serves as the initial, sole Trustee of the Trust. In Florida, the Declaration of Trust is specifically authorized by Statute. Not every state allows a Settlor to serve as sole Trustee of his or her own Trust.

Once a Revocable Trust is in existence, it may only be changed by the Settlor making an Amendment to the Trust. Extreme caution should be exercised here. The Settlor should never make handwritten alterations (additions or deletions) directly to the face of the Trust Instrument because in doing so, the entire Trust may be invalidated. A valid Trust Amendment requires a new writing, modifying (only) the affected language, which is executed with the same formalities as the original Trust Instrument. In Florida, since 1995, both the original Trust Instrument and all Amendments must be signed by the Settlor in the presence of **at least** two (2) attesting witnesses in order to be valid. No oral Trusts or Amendments to Trusts are permitted.

Advantages of the Revocable (Living) Trust

Privacy. The primary reason most often cited for adopting the Revocable Trust as the centerpiece of an individual's Estate Plan is that of privacy, meaning that all of the individual's innermost thoughts, i.e., who inherits what property or share of the Estate -- as spelled out in the Trust -- is kept confidential, as well as the nature and extent of the assets conveyed to the Trust during lifetime by the Settlor or Creator of the Trust. While it is true that all terms and provisions of a Revocable Trust are private -- because they are known only to the Settlor – under present Florida Probate Rules, the actual list of assets of a Decedent's Estate shown on the Probate Inventory is now sealed, thus, this information is not available for public inspection. However, the actual terms of every Will and Codicil admitted to Probate in the State of Florida continue to be open to the public. This tends to heighten the emotions of disgruntled heirs and promote Will contests and other Probate litigation. Clearly, if such omitted or slighted family members are unaware of the possible prejudice being visited upon them by the Decedent, fewer will resort to litigation in the Probate Court to redress their grievances. Thus, for persons who wish to reduce the likelihood of challenges to their Estate Plans, the use of a Revocable Trust or Declaration of Trust may be advisable.

Continuity of Management. The Revocable Trust provides the ideal entity or vehicle by which the Settlor's assets can be effectively and professionally managed and invested during the Settlor's lifetime, unimpaired by the possibility of sudden or gradual incapacity. The Settlor may delegate complete investment authority to a separate individual or corporate Trustee, or he or she may retain complete responsibility for management of all Trust assets and activities.

For the person who is physically unable, or who merely finds it inconvenient, to go back and forth to a safe deposit box, or to sign papers, monitor securities, or who is questionably disabled or incapacitated, the Revocable Trust provides substantial protection and security. The Revocable Trust permits the Settlor to observe the practical operations of the Trust's management by the selected Trustee. A Testamentary Trust, which arises under the person's Last Will and Testament, and takes effect only after the individual's death, offers the Testator no such opportunity to observe the management of his or her assets. With a Revocable Trust, the Settlor can observe the Trustee and/or remove the Trustee in order to ensure that the Trust will operate smoothly after his or her death. If the Settlor owns a business, has income-producing assets, or other assets that require daily supervision, he or she may ensure continuity by establishing appropriate systems and techniques within the Trust Instrument for their management and operation. The Settlor may also train a Co-Trustee or Successor or standby Trustee in the operation or management of his or her business and/or other assets. This observance of the Trustee or Co-Trustee helps the Settlor assess how the beneficiaries may react after the Settlor's death.

Consider the case of a wealthy northern retiree who comes to Florida where the lifestyle is more relaxed and the winters more conducive to his or her health and well being. Much of this person's property remains back in the "big city" or scattered in other states. Court proceedings for Probate in other jurisdictions (called "Ancillary Probate") are often complicated, time consuming and expensive. Executors (Personal Representatives) appointed under the person's Will may have to qualify in the foreign states, or, on the other hand, they may not be permitted to serve as Executor there. The person may also wish to have those advisors who guided him or her to financial security during his or her lifetime continue to do the same for his or her spouse and children following death.

Avoiding Guardianship/Conservatorship. Both the Revocable Trust and the Declaration of Trust provide methods for avoiding the delays, stigma and other related problems often associated with a formal court instituted and supervised Guardianship or Conservatorship procedure. For example, a Revocable Trust may provide that upon the occurrence of any one of the following events, the Co-Trustee or successor Trustee shall assume the full responsibility for the care and management of the Trust Estate:

1. The Settlor's written surrender of control;

2. The Settlor's unaccounted absence for a certain extended period of time;

3. Certification to the Trustee by one (1) or more named individuals (preferably physicians) that the Settlor can no longer make the decisions that are required or necessary to govern his or her finances and other personal affairs; or

4. Formal adjudication by a Court of competent jurisdiction that the Settlor is incapacitated due to mental or physical disabilities and thus requires the appointment of a Guardian or Conservator.

Avoiding Probate. All assets held in a Revocable Trust or a Declaration of Trust at the death of its Settlor avoid Probate, as these assets are not subject to administration. This arrangement not only reduces the costs of Probate (which in Florida are very modest, the current filing fee in Palm Beach County being approximately four hundred one dollars ($401), regardless of the value of the Estate), but more importantly, the Trust avoids the delays frequently associated with the transfer of assets which are encountered during the Probate Administration process. The successor Trustee continues with the management of the Trust without interruption or inconvenience to the beneficiaries who have immediate access to the continued flow of all income from the Trust. The process of locating, identifying and assembling the Probate assets is avoided when the Trust is successfully funded during the decedent's lifetime.

In addition, the Revocable Trust Instrument is not deposited with the Court, nor is the Trust's Schedule of Assets made a part of the public record. The Trust does not come under the supervision or jurisdiction of the Probate Court. In Florida, it is necessary to file an independent action or complaint with the Civil Division of the Circuit Court in order to invoke the Court's jurisdiction over an existing Trust. Similarly, the post-Probate administration of Testamentary Trusts (i.e., those created under a Will) is not supervised by the Florida Courts. It is not necessary to file and obtain Probate Court approval of the annual accounts of a Testamentary Trust. Thus, the laws of the State of Florida are very flexible when it comes to the administration of Trusts.

Recently, changes have been made to Florida's Trust Laws that may require that the Trustee of a deceased Florida resident's Revocable Trust file a Notice of Trust in a local newspaper and serve the same on reasonably ascertainable creditors of the deceased Settlor. Thus, trust assets are liable for the payment of a decedent's creditors, just as are Probate assets. However, this Notice procedure is advantageous because it allows the Trustee and beneficiaries to be reasonably certain that all of the decedent's financial obligations are paid, so that no creditors come forward in the future seeking payment of the decedent's debts.

Some problems can be eliminated or simplified by placing title to property located in different states in the name of and under the management of the Trustee of a single Revocable Trust which can continue to administer and distribute the Trust Estate smoothly, both before and after the Settlor's death.

Therefore, the typical use of a Revocable Trust is to avoid the necessity of having Ancillary or multiple Probate proceedings through the conveyance, IN TRUST, of the Settlor's foreign real estate (i.e., the real estate located in states other than Florida). By conveying the real estate, IN TRUST, the nature of the asset is changed to intangible personal property, and this allows Florida Law to govern or to take jurisdiction over the asset. In addition, for the Florida resident, the proper drafting of the Settlor's reserved powers retains for the Settlor and his or her family the Homestead real estate tax exemption, despite the transfer of title of the real estate to the Trust.

For the nonresident individual seeking to serve as a Florida Trustee, there are no Florida Laws which restrict or deny his or her designation or limit their ability to hold title to Florida property. If the person is capable of taking title to property for himself, he or she may take title to property as Trustee. The individual nonresident Trustee need not meet standards any different from those applicable to Florida residents who are Trustees of Florida property. As previously mentioned, such individuals are prohibited from being the Personal Representative under the Settlor's Last Will and Testament unless they are related to the Settlor/Testator in a certain degree of blood relationship. A Chart illustrating Chart of Legal Blood Relations (Consanguinity) appears as Exhibit VI to this book.

As for corporate Trustees, however, Florida Law is different. In Florida, there are severe limitations placed upon the activities that may be performed by the foreign (i.e., out-of-state) corporate Trustee. Some of these limitations include the following:

1. A testamentary Trustee (one serving as a Trustee under the decedent's Will) that is a foreign corporation may only receive bequests of money, intangible personal property and real property located in Florida, and perhaps may receive bequests of tangible personal property located in Florida. The property cannot come from a source other than the decedent.

2. When a Testamentary Trust is involved, the foreign corporate Trustee may sell, transfer or convey in Florida only money, intangible personal property and real property located in Florida and received as a bequest under the applicable Will.

3. A testamentary Trustee that is a foreign corporation may not act in Florida with respect to any property that it did not acquire as a bequest of money, intangible personal property or real property located in Florida.

4. The foreign corporate Trustee of a Revocable Trust may exercise its power in Florida over any Florida property *except* Florida real estate.

A Summary of the Advantages of
The Revocable (Living) Trust

1. The Trust and its Schedule of Assets do not become a part of the public Court record.

2.   Newspaper publicity about dispositive provisions, dollar amounts, and the identities of beneficiaries remembered or disinherited is avoided.

3.   Trust accounting proceedings need not be brought into Court.

4.   Publicity about litigation arising in Court accounting proceedings is avoided.

5.   Court procedures make it more difficult for disgruntled heirs to successfully contest a Trust than a Will, and it is easier for the Trustee to defend a Trust than to defend a Will.

6.   If an independent Trustee is selected, the Settlor is relieved of the day-to-day details of property management such as clipping coupons, going to a safe deposit box, exercising stock rights, watching for bond call notices, filing tax forms and keeping detailed records.

7.   No interruption in professional management of securities, family businesses, income flow or other property by reason of the Settlor's death or incapacity.

8.   No interruption in payment of the Settlor's medical and household bills, taxes, filing of necessary legal forms, or in caring for the Settlor's family in the event he or she becomes incapacitated.

9.   No delay occurs in paying debts, bills, expenses and benefits or in caring for the Settlor's family immediately after his or her death.

10.   The Settlor is able to observe other Trustees in actual operation while he or she is living, and can appraise their performance.

11.   The Settlor may employ a bank or trust company to act in a Fiduciary capacity and provide professional investment

management during his or her lifetime, often at commission rates comparable to investment advisory fees.

12. With respect to trust property, Personal Representative (Executor) fees and commissions are eliminated, attorneys' and appraisers' fees are reduced, Court filing fees are saved, and expenses of *Guardians Ad Litem* are eliminated.

13. Expensive Ancillary Estate Administration proceedings in multiple jurisdictions can be avoided.

14. The Settlor may choose the jurisdiction for administration of his or her Trust Estate, but not of his or her Probate Estate.

15. Specific assets can be segregated in trust during the Settlor's life and disposed of, intact, upon death in a different manner than the Settlor's other property.

16. The ultimate beneficiary of several life insurance policies naming the trust as beneficiary can be changed from time to time by making one amendment to trust, instead of separate changes in each policy beneficiary designation.

17. The Settlor is introduced to the advantages of the Trust device, and can consider the further use of Trusts of various types with potentially substantial Income and Estate Tax savings.

18. Annual Trust Accountings may not be required to be furnished to the Settlor by independent Trustee(s).

19. Probate of all assets transferred by the Settlor during lifetime to the Revocable Trust is completely avoided.

20. As with assets passing through Probate, the assets in a Revocable Trust receive a step-up in basis for Income Tax purposes at the death of the Settlor.

Federal Estate and Gift Tax

The term "Federal Estate Tax" is somewhat of a misnomer. Since 1976, there has been a *unified* Estate and Gift Tax system which, generally, taxes all transfers of property on the same basis, whether such transfers occur during one's lifetime (as gifts) or upon death (as bequests or devises). The reason for unification of these two (2) transfer taxes (Estate Tax and Gift Tax) is that if an individual gifts property during life, the value of such individual's Estate will have been depleted by the value of the property transferred and, therefore, be subject to less Estate Tax at death. Thus, Congress chose to tax the transfer of property under a single set of rules in order to avoid the possible abuses of the Federal Estate Tax Laws. A Chart illustrating current Federal Estate and Gift Tax amounts and rates appears as Exhibit VII to this book.

The following sections describe Estate Planning techniques frequently used to reduce Federal Transfer Taxes.

The Unified Credit

The Unified Credit directly offsets the tax liability owed on a person's Estate (i.e., property transferred at death) and on lifetime gifts. Federal Law requires the filing of a Federal Estate Tax Return (IRS Form 706) within nine (9) months of the decedent's death unless the Unified Credit exceeds the computed tax liability. It may be good practice, however, to file a Federal Estate Tax Return notwithstanding, so as to start the running of the statute of limitations. Lifetime gifts in excess of thirteen thousand dollars ($13,000) per person, per year, may reduce the amount of the Unified Credit available at the decedent's death. Under the Taxpayer Relief Act of 1997, the thirteen thousand dollar ($13,000) Annual Exclusion is indexed for inflation for gifts made after 1998.

The Unified Credit equates to an "Exemption Equivalent." The Exemption Equivalent is the value of the individual's Estate which is exempt from Estate Tax because of the Unified Credit. The Unified Credit may also represent the value of lifetime gifts which may be made without payment of Federal Gift Tax. The Unified Credit for Federal Gift Tax purposes directly offsets the amount of the Unified Credit available for Federal Estate Tax purposes. The Unified Credit for the year 2011 is five million dollars ($5,000,000), with an Exemption Equivalent of five million dollars ($5,000,000). In other words, if an individual dies in 2011 and leaves property having a total value of five million dollars ($5,000,000) or less for Federal Estate Tax purposes, there will be no Federal Estate Tax due, assuming no prior taxable gifts have been made. The excess taxable Estate (over $5,000,000) will be subject to a thirty-five percent (35%) Federal Estate Tax rate. Both the Federal Estate Tax rate and the Exemption Equivalent will remain at thirty-five percent (35%) and five million dollars ($5,000,000), respectively, through 2012.

Under the Tax Relief, Unemployment Insurance Reauthorization, and Job Creation Act of 2010, the Exemption Equivalent was scheduled to remain as follows:

Calendar Years	Exemption Equivalent
2011	$5 million
2012	$5 million

Note: Under the Act, the Federal Estate Tax Exemption is portable, meaning that if the first spouse dies and does not use up the five million dollar ($5,000,000) Exemption, the surviving spouse can use not only their own five million dollar ($5,000,000) Exemption but also what is left of the first-to-die spouse's Exemption. Additionally, the U.S. Gift Tax Exemption is equal to the Federal Estate Tax Exemption for 2011 and 2012 – meaning five million dollars ($5,000,000). Thereafter, under current law, the Federal Estate Tax is slated to return to its 2001 level with a one million dollar ($1,000,000) Exemption per individual and a top tax rate of fifty-five percent (55%).

It bears repeating that the amount of the Unified Credit used to offset Federal Gift Taxes directly reduces the amount of the Unified Credit available to pay Federal Estate Taxes. Thus, to the extent all or a portion of the Unified Credit remains at one's death, such amount will offset the Federal Estate Tax.

Preserving One's Unified Credit. The ownership of all of one's property jointly with his or her spouse (with the right of survivorship) wastes the Unified Credit of the first spouse to die, and may potentially result in more Federal Estate Tax being paid to the government than required. An amount representing the allowable Unified Credit should, generally, be placed in a Credit Shelter or By-Pass Trust, either during life or after death. This Trust can be structured so as to provide for the surviving spouse in substantially the same manner as if the property is owned by the surviving spouse outright. Putting the Exemption Equivalent amount *in Trust* can result in the value of the property not being included in the Taxable Estate of the surviving spouse. The surviving spouse's Unified Credit may then be applied against other property individually owned at death, thereby increasing the total Estate inherited by other family members.

The Marital Deduction

The Marital Deduction is based upon the premise that our Federal Government exempts from transfer taxes property which passes from one spouse to another, because it is anticipated that this same property will later be subject to transfer tax when transferred by the surviving spouse during life or at death, thereby increasing the total Estate inherited by other family members.

As long as a transfer between spouses is otherwise qualified, there is an **unlimited** Marital Deduction for Federal Estate and Gift Tax purposes. This means that an individual can transfer all of his or her assets to his or her spouse during lifetime as a gift, or leave his or her entire Estate to his or her surviving spouse at death, and totally avoid any Federal Gift or Estate Tax. However, as previously stated, this may result in the waste of the Unified Credit. If the spouse inherits an Estate of significant size and does not remarry, or remarries without transferring the property to the second spouse, there may be a very substantial tax due at the time of the death of the surviving spouse. This may be compounded by the fact that the surviving spouse may have property of his or her own. Any inherited property may push the surviving spouse's Estate into a higher Federal Estate Tax bracket, thereby causing more tax to be paid. Therefore, the Marital Deduction should not be "over-funded."

Utilization of a QTIP Trust

The Economic Recovery Act of 1981 created the Qualified Terminable Interest Property (QTIP) Trust. A QTIP Trust provision drafted as part of an Estate Plan can be very useful for the individual who would like to assure the welfare of a surviving spouse, but control who is ultimately to receive the property upon the death of the surviving spouse. Under the previous law, it was impossible to provide a lifetime income interest to a surviving spouse, direct which persons ultimately receive the remainder, **and** qualify the transfer for the Marital Deduction in the Estate of the first spouse to die. A QTIP Trust provides a surviving spouse with all income therefrom for life but the property in Trust will not pass as part of the surviving spouse's separate Estate. Instead, such property passes to those persons as directed by the first spouse to die. Thus, it is an ideal arrangement for second marriage situations because a spouse can obtain a Marital Deduction for property held in a QTIP Trust arrangement (whereby all income goes to the surviving spouse), but the property itself passes to the family (i.e., children) of the first spouse to die upon the surviving spouse's death.

The Unified Credit and Marital Deduction can work together to eliminate Federal Estate Taxes at the death of the first spouse. This is illustrated by the following Chart.

Estate of the first spouse is divided upon death:

MARITAL DEDUCTION PORTION (Estate in excess of the Unified Credit Equivalent)	CREDIT SHELTER PORTION (Up to the Unified Credit Equivalent) ($5,000,000 in assets in 2011/2012)
No Tax due upon death of first spouse	No Tax due upon death of first spouse

Upon death of the first spouse:

Held in Trust OR distributed outright to the surviving spouse	Held in Trust for the surviving spouse
Included in the surviving spouse's Taxable Estate	**Not included** in the surviving spouse's Taxable Estate

Upon the death of the surviving spouse:
Distributed to children, family members or other beneficiaries

Generation-Skipping Transfer Tax

Prior to enactment of the Generation-Skipping Transfer (GST) Tax in 1976, it was possible to transfer the use and enjoyment of property or the income therefrom to children without inclusion of the property in their Taxable Estates. As a result, upon the death of the children, the property could pass to grandchildren or lower generations without imposition of additional transfer tax. For example, a parent could establish a Trust at his or her death, directing that all of the income from such Trust be paid to the parent's child for his or her lifetime. At the child's death, the Trust property would be distributed to the parent's grandchildren. Because the child had a mere income interest for life, which was extinguished at his or her death, no part of the Trust was included in the child's Gross Estate for Federal Estate Tax purposes. Thus, one level of transfer tax (Estate or Gift) could be "skipped." The ability to "skip" a generation for tax purposes is now severely limited.

Under current law, in addition to the Federal Estate or Gift Tax, a Generation-Skipping Transfer Tax applies to transfers to persons who are two or more generations below that of the Transferor (i.e., grandchildren).

The Generation-Skipping Transfer Tax is imposed at a rate equal to the highest Federal Estate Tax rate (presently thirty-five percent (35%) in 2011/2012) as shown in the Table below. However, every individual is entitled to transfer the full amount of their Exemption for Generation-Skipping Transfers shown below. This Exemption Amount may be allocated to gifts made during life or to transfers at death. Certain transfers qualifying for the thirteen thousand dollar ($13,000) Annual Gift Tax Exclusion are also excluded from the Generation-Skipping Transfer Tax. In addition, direct payments for a donee's tuition or for medical expenses are also excluded from the GST Tax.

In the example above, at the child's death, a Generation-Skipping Transfer Tax would be payable out of the Trust assets, at the thirty-five percent (35%) tax bracket. If the parent had made an outright gift or bequest to the grandchild through the parent's Will or Trust, the GST Tax would apply **in addition to** the Federal Estate Tax. As stated above, GST Taxation is subject to the dollar Exemption(s) shown below and other transfer tax exclusions.

GENERATION-SKIPPING TRANSFER TAX RATES

Current Generation-Skipping Transfer Tax Rates *	
2011	35%
2012	35%

Estate and GST Tax Exemption *	
2011	$5,000,000
2012	$5,000,000

* Current Exemption amounts and marginal Estate Tax rates may change after 2012 depending upon future legislation passed by Congress. Presently, after 2012, the Federal Estate Tax is slated to return to its 2001 level with a one million dollar ($1,000,000) Exemption per individual and a top rate of fifty-five percent (55%).

Completed gifts of property may totally remove the value of such property from an individual's potential Taxable Estate. A gift is a transfer of property for less than "full and adequate consideration." A Federal Gift Tax is normally assessed on the value of such a transfer. The Unified Credit can be used to offset transfer taxes during life *or* at death. The best use of the Unified Credit is to use such credit to offset the value of lifetime gifts of *appreciating* property. This technique shelters the transfer of more property and is more advantageous than if highly-appreciated property is held until death. The following should be considered in such a program of planned giving.

The Annual Gift Tax Exclusion. Individuals, and certain business entities, can transfer up to thirteen thousand dollars ($13,000) annually to each of any number of persons without current Gift Taxation and without using any portion of the Donor's Unified Credit. If property is owned individually by a spouse, the other spouse may elect to join in the making of the gift to a third party, with each spouse being considered to have made one-half (½) of the gift, under the concept of "gift-splitting." As such, twenty-six thousand dollars ($26,000) of property owned by a married couple may be given to each of any number of persons (typically their children) free of Federal Gift Tax. This is true even though the property is legally owned only by one spouse. Annual Exclusion gifts may also be made by one spouse to the other using an Irrevocable Trust, with the couple's children being the ultimate (remainder) beneficiaries. Amounts gifted in excess of the Annual Exclusion reduce the transferor's Unified Credit.

Under the Act, for 2011 and 2012, all Gift Tax rates will mirror the Federal Estate Tax rates, as follows:

Highest Gift Tax Rates	
2011	35%
2012	35%

As mentioned earlier, Florida has no separate State Gift Tax which is payable upon transfers by bona fide Florida residents.

Payment of Tuition/Medical Expenses. Individuals may make unlimited gifts for tuition to an educational institution, and for medical expenses, on behalf of another, without incurring Federal Gift Tax. However, such gifts must be made directly to the educational or medical institution. Thus, reimbursement for such payments does not comply with the requirements for exclusion. The exclusion for payment of another's tuition does not extend to books, room and board, or other expenses relating to education.

This exclusion is *in addition to* the thirteen thousand dollar ($13,000) Annual Gift Tax Exclusion. Also, the Generation-Skipping Transfer Tax does not apply to such gifts.

Thus, the payment of another's tuition and medical expenses is an excellent method of paying such expenses for children and/or grandchildren while reducing one's Estate and avoiding one or more levels of Federal transfer taxes.

Section 529 Plans. New Estate Planning opportunities exist under qualified state tuition programs (sometimes called "Section 529 Plans" because they are established under Internal Revenue Code Section 529) which receive favorable treatment for Gift, Estate and Income Tax purposes. Individual program accounts can be established for each intended beneficiary, e.g., child, grandchild, niece or nephew, among others. Amounts may then be withdrawn from the accounts for "qualified higher education expenses," defined broadly to include tuition, fees, books, supplies, and equipment required for post-secondary education, as well as qualifying room and board. Effective for 2002, private colleges and universities may establish their own qualified tuition programs.

However, for property law purposes, the Donor is treated as the owner of the plan, and contributions qualify for the thirteen thousand dollar ($13,000) Annual Exclusion for Federal Gift Tax purposes. Moreover, at the Donor's election, excess contributions made in a single year may be carried forward (ratably) for five (5) years. For example, a sixty-five thousand dollar ($65,000) contribution in 2011 may be treated as five (5) annual thirteen thousand dollar ($13,000) contributions made in 2011 through 2016, each of which qualifies for the thirteen thousand dollar ($13,000) Annual Exclusion. At the Donor's death, no part of the program account (other than the excess contributions carried forward, if any) is subject to Federal Estate Tax.

Beginning in 2002, distributions made from state qualified tuition plans and used to pay for qualified educational expenses are tax-free, i.e., no part of the distribution is subject to Income Tax. Beginning in 2004, distributions from qualified tuition plans established by private colleges and universities and used to pay qualified educational expenses are tax-free.

Irrevocable Trusts

Lifetime transfers to an Irrevocable Trust may be used to reduce Estate Taxes.

An Irrevocable Trust may also be utilized by the person who would like to remove the value of certain property from his or her Taxable Estate, but at the same time would like to restrict the use or enjoyment of the property by the recipient (i.e., perhaps the recipient is a spendthrift, has a problem marriage or, because of his or her profession, is at high risk for liability).

Various provisions can be drafted into the Trust document so as to restrict the recipient's outright control over the property, while insuring that the recipient has the right to the income of the property and/or access to Trust principal under certain desired circumstances.

Caution is required, however, because transfers to Irrevocable Trusts cannot be reversed, and the terms of the Trust cannot be changed once executed.

Charitable Planned Giving

If an individual desires to benefit a church, synagogue, educational institution, hospital or other charitable organization, charitable giving may be as fundamental a part of overall Estate Planning as providing for a spouse and children. Even for those with lesser charitable inclinations, charitable giving offers many Estate, Gift and Income Tax advantages.

Outright Charitable Gifts. The simplest form of charitable giving is through outright gifts of cash or other property to one or more charities. Such gifted property fully qualifies for a Gift Tax Charitable Deduction and is removed from the Donor's potential Taxable Estate. Moreover, such a gift gives rise to an Income Tax Charitable Deduction. Generally, a current Income Tax Deduction is available for the full value of the gifted property up to fifty percent (50%) of the Donor's Adjusted Gross Income. For a gift of an appreciated capital asset, the deduction is allowed up to thirty percent (30%) of the Donor's Adjusted Gross Income. In both cases, there is a five (5) year carryover of any unused part of the deduction. By giving away highly-appreciated property to a charity, one can avoid the Capital Gains Tax on a future sale of such property.

Charitable Remainder Trusts. An individual may create a Trust for the ultimate benefit of one or more charities, while reserving an annuity for life or a term of years, payable from the property donated to the Trust. At the end of the term of years or at the death of the annuitant, the remainder passes to the charity named in the Trust.

Alternatively, such a Trust can be established at one's death, with an annuity from the property payable to a spouse or child for life or for a term of years, with the property passing to the charity upon the death of the annuitant or the end of the term of years.

This Trust has the advantage of removing the property held therein from the Donor's Estate. Note: Recent IRS Rulings suggest that it may be necessary for a surviving spouse to "waive" any interest in a Charitable Remainder Trust created for the benefit of another to preserve the anticipated deduction for tax purposes.

Selecting Property to Give. The goal of most Estate Planning techniques is to reduce future Estate Tax at a minimum (or no) current Gift Tax cost. Property with a relatively low present value, but with great potential appreciation, is the most advantageous property to give away. Obviously, the lower the current value and the higher the potential for appreciation, the better. It may not be wise to gift property which is already highly appreciated, and on which a large Capital Gains Tax would be recognized if sold because a Donee takes the Donor's tax basis in the property gifted. This is to be contrasted with property acquired from a decedent, which receives a "step-up" in tax basis in a beneficiary's hands, following the death of the property owner. Thus, all appreciation prior to the property owner's death will forever go untaxed.

The Irrevocable Life Insurance Trust

The Irrevocable Life Insurance Trust (ILIT) has been used by Estate Planners for many years. The advent of the unlimited Estate Tax Marital Deduction substantially increased the amount of property that can be passed free of Estate Tax to the surviving spouse. And, if properly arranged, a married couple may transfer twice the amount of the Unified Credit Equivalent to family members without incurring any Federal Estate Tax liability. In larger Estates, proper planning can greatly reduce the Federal Estate Tax liability, but cannot completely eliminate such tax. The ILIT is the best way to provide liquidity to pay the reduced Estate Taxes, especially upon the death of the surviving spouse.

Generally, the ILIT is an irrevocable Trust created during the lifetime of the Creator of the Trust, called the Grantor. Upon creation, the Trustee purchases an insurance policy on the life of the Grantor. Alternatively, an ILIT may own a joint and survivor policy insuring the lives of multiple Grantors (i.e., husband and wife). The Grantors may then make annual gifts to the Trustee of the Trust on behalf of the Trust beneficiaries. The Trustee, in turn, may use such gifted funds to pay annual policy premiums.

The ILIT may also contain specific provisions intended to optimize the tax benefits of the Trust. Such provisions include the use of a beneficiary's demand withdrawal right, or "Crummey" power, so that most, if not all, of the annual premium payments do not create Federal Gift Tax consequences. In addition, an ILIT owning a policy on one spouse's life may contain a provision giving the Grantor's spouse a Special Power of Appointment to distribute the life insurance proceeds, following the insured Grantor's death, to specified family members during the Grantor's spouse's lifetime. And, in larger Estates, the ILIT may be used in the format of a "Dynasty Trust" -- one scheduled to continue for several generations into the future.

Where a Grantor transfers an existing life insurance policy on his or her life to the ILIT, he or she must survive three (3) years from the date of such transfer to ensure that the policy is not taxable in his or her Estate. With an ILIT, the Grantor can ensure a source of financial support for his or her spouse without causing the inclusion of the insurance proceeds in *either* spouse's Taxable Estate. Also, an ILIT can be a source of liquidity to both Estates without causing a Federal Estate Tax liability, by giving the Trustee the power to make loans to the Estates of the respective spouses for these purposes, or to purchase assets from their Estates at finally determined Estate Tax values.

The ILIT also allows the Grantor to avoid Gift Tax consequences on all but extremely large life insurance policies. In addition, the Grantor can provide the flexibility to meet unforeseen major changes in his or her family's situation by utilizing specially tailored Trust provisions capable of anticipating changed circumstances.

An increasingly common and advantageous technique is to combine an ILIT with a Charitable Remainder Trust. This is known as the "Wealth Replacement Technique." The Trusts are coordinated so that the income interest retained by the Donor from the Charitable Remainder Trust may be used to pay insurance policy premiums by gifting such amounts to the ILIT. This technique allows the Grantor to reduce his or her Taxable Estate by means of the charitable deduction from the Charitable Remainder Trust, provide liquidity for the payment of Estate Taxes through the ILIT, and maintain the value of the family's inheritance.

Grantor Retained Interest Trust

Under prior law, an individual could transfer assets into a Trust, retaining a right to all of the income for life, and designating children or other beneficiaries to receive the remainder after the Grantor's death. The Grantor would have made a gift of the value of the property transferred **less** the retained right to income, determined actuarially. Thus, a Gift Tax may have been payable on a relatively small gift. Moreover, the Grantor could maximize this technique by investing the Trust assets for growth, rather than income production. This resulted in small income payments, and a transfer of highly appreciated assets, at low Gift Tax cost. Congress severely restricted this technique in the early 1990s by treating the **entire value** of the property transferred to such a Trust as a Taxable Gift. However, this gifting technique may continue to be utilized through the use of certain specific types of Trusts.

The three (3) allowable Grantor Retained Interest Trusts are the following: the Grantor Retained Annuity Trust (GRAT), the Grantor Retained Unitrust (GRUT), and the Personal Residence Trust discussed below. These types of Trusts allow a Grantor to remove property and appreciation from the Estate, while retaining an interest in the Trust. The Grantor may not retain the right to all of the income from such Trust, but rather an annuity based on a specific dollar amount or percentage of the Trust assets. In the GRAT or GRUT, the annuity is payable for a term of years, usually from five (5) to ten (10) years. At the end of the annuity term, the remainder is either distributed to, or held in, further Trust for the benefit of, the ultimate beneficiaries.

The Grantor will have made a gift of a portion of the fair market value of the property transferred to the Trust **minus** the Grantor's retained interest based on the term of years and IRS interest rates. Thus, the longer the term of the retained annuity, the smaller the amount of the gift to the remainder beneficiaries.

It should be noted that if the Grantor dies before the term of the annuity ends, the entire Trust will be included in the Grantor's Gross Estate for Federal Estate Tax purposes.

Personal Residence Trust

The Personal Residence Trust is simply a GRAT or GRUT to which the Grantor transfers ownership of his or her personal residence. The Grantor retains an interest in the Trust -- the right to occupy the residence -- for a term of years, usually five (5) to ten (10) years. Because there is an actual transfer of property, there may be a Gift Tax due at the inception of the Trust. However, such Gift Tax could be wholly or partially offset by the remaining Unified Credit of the Grantor.

Basically, the amount of the gift is determined by subtracting the value of the Grantor's retained interest (determined actuarially) from the fair market value of the property. At the end of the Trust term, the property passes to the remainder beneficiaries, according to the terms of the Trust. The primary advantage of the Personal Residence Trust is that by paying a relatively small Gift Tax currently, an individual may remove the entire value of his or her residence, as well as future appreciation thereon, from his or her Estate.

If the Grantor outlives the term of the Trust, the residence will no longer be an asset of the Gross Estate for Federal Estate Tax purposes. So as not to draw scrutiny from the Internal Revenue Service, the Grantor may not continue to use the residence, unless he or she pays fair market value rent to the Trustee or beneficiaries, as the case may be. These rental payments serve to further reduce the Grantor's Taxable Estate.

During the term of the Trust, the Grantor continues to be treated as the Owner of the property for other tax purposes. Thus, the Grantor must still pay real property taxes, but also can take advantage of any available State or Federal Tax deductions or credits available by reason of owning such property.

The downside to the Personal Residence Trust is that if the Grantor predeceases the term of the Trust, the residence is included in the Grantor's Taxable Estate for Federal Estate Tax purposes. In actuality, this leaves the Grantor in no worse position than if the Trust had never been established, except that the opportunity for a step-up in the cost basis of the property at the Grantor's death is lost.

The Internal Revenue Service allows an individual to establish a maximum of two (2) Personal Residence Trusts, and each such Trust may only own one (1) personal residence.

The Family Limited Partnership

One of the most popular Estate Planning techniques since the 1990's involves the establishment of a Family Limited Partnership (FLP).

By transferring assets to such a Partnership, a senior family member may take advantage of valuation discounts for Gift and Estate Tax purposes. The FLP is a means of transferring assets to lower generations of family members, at a reduced transfer tax cost.

Property such as stocks and bonds, real estate or other limited partnership interests, may be transferred into a new partnership entity. Transfer of assets to a partnership may generally be accomplished Income Tax-free.

A limited partnership contains both Limited Partner interests and General Partner interests. The General Partner is in charge of managing the partnership assets and the day-to-day affairs of the Partnership. The Limited Partners have no say in or control over the Partnership's operations, but merely possess a right to a percentage of partnership profits. Initially, the transferor holds a majority of the partnership interests as a Limited Partner. The transferor then makes gifts of his or her Limited Partner interests to children, grandchildren, and/or Trusts for their benefit.

Gifts of Limited Partner interests are discounted for their *lack of marketability*, and their status as *minority interests*. These discounts are based on the lack of a ready market to determine the value of Family Partnership interests, and also the Limited Partner's lack of control over the management of the partnership. These discounts may result in the Gifted Limited Partner interests being valued at ten percent (10%) to forty percent (40%) less than the value of the underlying partnership property. For example, if a twenty-five percent (25%) discount is utilized, a gift of Limited Partner interests which equal seventeen thousand three hundred thirty-four dollars ($17,344) worth of underlying property is valued at only thirteen thousand dollars ($13,000), thereby qualifying for the Annual Gift Tax Exclusion.

This gifting process may be repeated annually. In addition, the transferor may utilize his or her Unified Credit to make gifts of larger Limited Partner interests. At the death of the transferor, his or her remaining partnership interest may also be discounted for Federal Estate Tax purposes.

In order to maximize the use of valuation discounts, a professional appraiser should be retained. A well-documented appraisal provides support for valuation discounts in case such are questioned by the Internal Revenue Service, which is likely based upon recent Internal Revenue Service announced protocol and procedure.

The transferor, either alone or with one or more individuals, usually serves as General Partner of the FLP. Thus, the transferor may control the partnership assets for the remainder of his or her lifetime. It is generally recommended that there be one or more General Partners in order to maximize Federal Estate Tax discounts at the death of a General Partner who also owns a

Limited Partner interest. In that case, the transferor may serve as Managing General Partner, to ensure the retention of control.

A partnership is a "pass-through" entity for Income Tax purposes. Thus, there is no tax due at the entity level (although an informational tax return is required to be filed). Rather, the individual partners are liable for Income Tax on their proportionate shares of partnership income. Partnership income is allocated to the partners annually, based on their percentage interests. Thus, the Family Limited Partnership is a means of shifting income to family members who may be in lower tax brackets than the transferor. Also, the General Partner may be given the ability to decide how much income is actually distributed to the individual partners. In this way, the transferor may gift an asset (partnership interest) to children and grandchildren, without allowing them to receive all of the income earned from such asset, currently.

A Florida Limited Partnership must file a Certificate of Limited Partnership with the Florida Department of State. An initial filing fee is required, currently one thousand dollars ($1,000). In addition, an Annual Report is required to be filed, together with a modest annual filing fee (namely, four hundred eleven dollars and twenty-five cents ($411.25) filing fee and eighty-eight dollars and seventy-five cents ($88.75) supplemental fee, or five hundred dollars ($500.00 total).

Since its repeal in 2006, intangible personal property (i.e., stocks, bonds, notes, etc.) held in a Family Limited Partnership will not be subject to the Florida Intangible Personal Property Tax.

Consider the following example: John Doe contributes stock with a market value of eight hundred twelve thousand five hundred dollars ($812,500) to the Doe Family Limited Partnership. John Doe retains a two percent (2%) interest as General Partner and forty-five percent (45%) interest as Limited Partner. John gives his wife, Jane, a forty-five percent (45%) Limited Partner interest, (which can be accomplished Gift Tax-free using the Marital Deduction) and gives each of his two children and two grandchildren two percent (2%) Limited Partner interests. Each two percent (2%) interest, without any discount, would be valued for Gift Tax purposes at sixteen thousand two hundred fifty dollars ($16,250). However, by applying a twenty percent (20%) valuation discount, each gift is valued at thirteen thousand dollars ($13,000) for Gift Tax Purposes, equal to the Annual Exclusion amount for such gifts. Thus, John would have shifted sixty-five thousand dollars ($65,000) of his assets to his children and grandchildren with no Gift Tax cost. Moreover, such amounts will not be subject to Federal Estate Tax in John's Estate. Jane may also gift her Limited Partner interests, with the same Gift and Estate Tax benefits. Thus, John and Jane, together, may transfer one hundred thirty thousand dollars ($130,000) of assets annually with no Gift Tax.

In addition, each child and grandchild would thereafter be entitled to two percent (2%) of all Partnership distributions, which may be made at the discretion of the General Partner. Gifts in later years would further reduce the value of John's Partnership interests, while increasing the interests of his children and grandchildren. At John's death, his remaining interest may be discounted for Federal Estate Tax purposes.

Similar Federal Estate Tax savings may be achieved through the use of a Limited Liability Company.

Caution should be exercised in using a Family Limited Partnership because recent Court cases brought by the Internal Revenue Service successfully challenged discounts sought by Estates of taxpayers who established and funded the Family Limited Partnership shortly before death, calling the same a sham transaction.

Retirement Plans

Retirement Plans, such as IRAs, are excellent devices for achieving tax-free growth. However, because Retirement Plans may be subject to Income Tax *and* Estate Tax, as well as various Penalty Taxes, proper planning is required to limit the imposition of these taxes, and allow as much property as possible to be passed on to future generations.

The Beneficiary Designation is at the center of planning for retirement plan distributions. The Beneficiary Designation determines not only *who* will receive the benefits following the Plan Owner's death, but also what the *amount* of the minimum annual distributions, and the *length of time* over which the Plan benefits are payable. Thus, the Beneficiary Designation plays a greater role in Retirement Plans than for life insurance and annuities.

Some Plans, typically employer-provided plans -- but not IRAs -- require that the participant's spouse receive a minimum amount of benefits if such spouse survives the participant. In such case, one other than a spouse may not be named as Designated Beneficiary unless the spouse provides a consent and waiver, as required.

Every Plan Owner must begin taking distributions from his or her retirement plan, generally by age seventy and one-half (70½). Thereafter, there is a minimum amount which must be distributed annually. The failure to withdraw the minimum amount, or the withdrawal of greater than a specified amount, results in a Penalty Tax imposed on the distribution. If a Plan Owner dies with too large a plan balance, a Penalty Tax will be imposed on such accumulation, in addition to the Estate Tax.

Disclaimers

Florida Law permits a beneficiary of a Will or a Trust to "Disclaim" (refuse to accept) all or a part of their inheritance. To be valid, a Disclaimer must be in writing and executed with all the formalities required in conveyances of real property, i.e., signed in the presence of two (2) attesting witnesses and a Notary Public. In addition, it must be filed with the Clerk of the Probate Court within nine (9) months of the decedent's death and/or delivered to the Trustee/Personal Representative where applicable. The disclaiming beneficiary is treated as though he or she had predeceased the decedent, and the property or share of the

◊ ——————————————————— ◊

Estate which has been disclaimed then passes to the next beneficiary entitled to inherit under the Will or Trust. Thus, it is possible for a decedent's family to, in effect, "rewrite" the decedent's Will or Trust to a certain extent so as to pass property to other family members who may be next in line to receive this inheritance. With proper advice, a Disclaimer may be utilized to reduce or eliminate Estate Taxes, rearrange funds within a family, cure a defective term or provision of a Will or Trust, and increase or reduce the amount of a Marital Deduction, all without the imposition of any Gift Taxes.

Also, under certain circumstances, it is possible to Disclaim non-Probate forms of conveyances such as jointly-owned property (with the right of survivorship), life insurance proceeds, "in-trust-for" bank accounts and more. As such, the Disclaimer is an extremely valuable post-mortem Estate Planning tool, but it should only be utilized after a careful appraisal of all tax and non-tax considerations involved.

SPOUSAL RIGHTS

There are certain statutory rights afforded to a surviving spouse under Florida Law which ensure that some provision will be made for the spouse despite the terms of a deceased spouse's Last Will and Testament. One such right or interest is the spouse's "Elective Share," which specifies the share of the decedent's Probate Estate to which a surviving spouse is entitled.

Pursuant to Florida Law, which was amended to be effective for all decedents dying on or after October 1, 2001, the surviving spouse's Elective Share is equal to thirty percent (30%) of the Elective Estate, which *includes* (1) the decedent's Probate Estate; (2) the decedent's interest in accounts and securities held in joint ownership with right of survivorship, pay-on-death (POD), transfer-on-death (TOD) or in-trust-for (ITF) arrangements; (3) the decedent's interest in joint ownership arrangements for property other than accounts and securities; (4) property held in arrangements that are revocable by the decedent alone or in conjunction with another person; (5) property transferred by the decedent with either a retained right to income or if principal could be distributed to the decedent by someone other than the spouse; (6) the decedent's interest in the cash surrender value of life insurance policies on the decedent's life; (7) death benefits under the decedent's retirement plans; (8) property transferred as a gift by the decedent within one [1] year of death, except for certain excluded gifts; and (9) property transferred or segregated during lifetime to satisfy the Elective Share.

The deadline to file a claim for the Elective Share is the *earlier* of (i) six (6) months after first publication of the Notice to Creditors in the decedent's Estate, or (ii) two (2) years after the date of the decedent's death.

Thus, the election to "take against the Will" is an affirmative action on the part of the surviving spouse and does not arise automatically.

In addition to the Elective Share provisions described above, a surviving spouse is entitled to certain additional property set apart from the deceased spouse's Probate Estate and held for the benefit of the surviving spouse. Such additional property includes:

1. The Family Homestead, which derives its existence from Article X, Section 4 of the Florida Constitution, places certain restrictions on the right of a decedent to devise or "will" Homestead property while the decedent-owner's spouse or minor children are living. There is no affirmative action required by the surviving spouse as a prerequisite to the claiming of such right to Homestead. Pursuant to a recent Florida Constitutional Amendment, Homestead now attaches to all real property which is owned and resided on by a natural person at the time of death, whether such person is the "head of a family" or not.

2. Certain exempt personal property owned by the deceased spouse, such as household furniture, furnishings and appliances in the decedent's usual place of abode up to a net value of ten thousand dollars ($10,000), plus all automobiles held in the decedent's name and regularly used by the decedent or members of the immediate family as their personal (i.e., non-business) automobiles.

3. Personal effects of the deceased spouse up to a net value of one thousand dollars ($1,000), unless the personal effects are otherwise disposed of by Will or Codicil.

4. Florida Prepaid College Program contracts and Florida College Savings Agreements established under Florida Law.

5. A reasonable family allowance where the deceased spouse is domiciled in Florida at the time of death and is survived by a spouse or lineal heirs whom the deceased spouse was obligated to support or who were, in fact, being supported by the deceased spouse. The amount that may be awarded by the Court as a family allowance is limited to a total of eighteen thousand dollars ($18,000).

It should be mentioned briefly that upon dissolution of a marriage, Florida's Equitable Distribution Statute applies to the division of property. This Statute authorizes the Court in a divorce proceeding in Florida to "fairly" distribute marital assets based on several factors including contribution to the marriage, economic circumstances and duration of the marriage. Assets acquired separately by either spouse through non-spousal gifts or bequests, or through devise and descent from Estates of family members, are **not** considered marital assets for purposes of this Statute and are thus protected from the claims of a divorcing spouse provided they are not commingled.

Florida, like other jurisdictions, allows spouses to waive the statutory rights granted to them in each other's respective Estate. The waivers generally take the form of either a Prenuptial (before marriage) or Postnuptial (after marriage) Agreement and, to be enforceable, certain minimum statutory formalities must be observed. Florida Law does not require a full disclosure of the nature and value of one's Estate prior to the execution of a *Pre*nuptial Agreement, although it is a better practice to do so. The opposite of this rule holds true in the *Post*nuptial situation. In the latter circumstance, Florida Law requires a "fair disclosure" be made by the parties as to the value of the assets which constitute each other's respective Estates.

In each of the foregoing circumstances, the marital agreements must be executed with the same formalities required for the execution of a valid Will. In other words, such marital agreements shall not be binding or enforceable unless in writing and signed by the respective party in the presence of two (2) attesting witnesses. Ordinarily, to be enforceable, such marital agreements must contain all the essential elements of a contract such as, but not limited to, an offer, acceptance and consideration in money or money's worth, or the performance or non-performance of some act. However, in the case of marital agreements, generally no consideration other than the execution of the agreement and the consummation of the marriage is necessary to ensure its validity.

Effective on October 1, 2007, under the Uniform Premarital Agreement Act, which applies only to proceedings under the Florida Family Law Rules of Procedure, parties to a Premarital Agreement may contract with respect to, *inter alia*, the disposition of property upon separation, marital dissolution or death which includes the making of a Will, Trust or other arrangement to carry out the provisions of the Agreement. The term "property" is broadly defined to include an interest, present or future, legal or equitable, vested or contingent, in real or personal property, tangible or intangible, including income and earnings, both active and passive. The Act further provides that after marriage, a Premarital Agreement may be amended, revoked or abandoned only by a written agreement signed by the parties and is enforceable without consideration. The Act further provides that a Premarital Agreement is not enforceable in an action proceeding under the Florida Family Law Rules of Procedure if the party against whom enforcement is sought proves that:

1. The party did not execute the Agreement voluntarily;

2. The Agreement was the product of fraud, duress, coercion, or overreaching; or

3. The Agreement was unconscionable when it was executed and, before execution of that Agreement, that party (i) was not provided a fair and reasonable disclosure of the property or financial obligations of the other party; (ii) did not voluntarily and expressly waive, in writing, any right to disclosure of the property or financial obligations of the other party beyond the disclosure provided; and (iii) did not have, or reasonably could not have had, an adequate knowledge of the property or financial obligations of the other party.

ASSET PROTECTION PLANNING

Asset Protection Planning is a specialized form of Estate Planning for those whose wealth may be exposed to risk of loss for any number of reasons. Doctors, lawyers, business owners and real estate developers are some of the types of occupations which are frequently exposed to personal liability. Also, in cases of divorce and actions by personal creditors, individuals may wish to protect their assets. This type of advance planning is increasingly important because once liability attaches to an individual, it is too late for any meaningful planning. "Fraudulent Conveyance" laws prohibit transfers of assets following the determination of liability, and even prior to such a determination, where the possibility of liability is imminent.

Asset Protection Planning takes on many different forms — from the simple to the complex. On the simple end, holding assets in joint ownership form may prevent the creditors of one of the joint owners from reaching the joint property. Creditors of Trust beneficiaries (except the Settlor in the case of a Declaration of Trust or Revocable Trust) may be unable to reach the underlying Trust assets where a "spendthrift clause" is included in the Trust Instrument. In some circumstances, a Spendthrift Trust may be established with its main purpose being to shelter the beneficiary's interest from the reach of his or her creditors. Also, a Discretionary Trust may be established, whereby distributions may be made to the beneficiary only at the discretion of the Trustee. This type of Trust prevents creditors of the beneficiary from forcing the Trustee to make distributions, but allows the Trustee flexibility to make distributions in case the creditors retreat from their collection efforts and initiatives.

The most well-known protection for property available to Florida residents is the Florida Homestead Exemption. Article X, Section 4 of the Florida Constitution provides that the Homestead of a Florida resident (and natural person) is exempt from forced sale under the process of any Court. There is no limitation as to the *value* of the residence. The only exception to this rule is for taxes and assessments, and voluntary liens for the purchase, improvement or repair of the Property. The term "Homestead" is defined as one-half (½) acre of contiguous land within a municipality or one hundred sixty (160) acres of contiguous land outside a municipality.

Personal property is also exempt up to the value of one thousand dollars ($1,000) under Florida Law.

Both of these Exemptions inure to the benefit of the surviving spouse or heirs of the owner.

Other types of property which offer Asset Protection features are life insurance policies, annuities and retirement plans.

Asset ownership by spouses as Tenants by Entirety may also be advantageous as a creditor of only one spouse has no rights to assets held as Tenants by Entirety. In other words, only a creditor of both spouses has rights in Tenants by Entirety assets. This form of ownership may be desirable in situations where one spouse's occupation may subject them to significant liability such as Doctors and Lawyers.

Asset Protection Planning may take on a more complex nature through the use of specialized entities as a means of holding title to assets. The Family Limited Partnership, discussed above, provides Asset Protection for Limited Partners. The transfer of assets to a Partnership results in the ownership of a Partnership interest, rather than an undivided portion of the underlying assets. Generally, creditors of one Limited Partner may not reach the assets of the Partnership or of another Limited Partner. Likewise, the creditors of the Partnership may not reach the other individually owned assets of a Limited Partner. Rather, such creditors must be content with a "charging order," merely entitling them to an interest in Partnership profits *when actually distributed to the Limited Partner.*

Asset Protection Trusts (APTs) may now be established in states which recently enacted favorable legislation ensuring special protection from creditors for Trust beneficiaries. States which now favor APTs are Alaska, Colorado, Delaware, Missouri, Nevada and Rhode Island.

The most complex, and successful, asset protection device is the Offshore Trust. As its name implies, this type of Trust has its situs in a foreign jurisdiction, outside of the United States. The principal basis of their protected status is that a judgment creditor in the United States cannot reach the assets of a Trust established outside the United States unless a Treaty exists between the two (2) countries that permits the enforcement/collection of civil judgments in the non-US jurisdiction. Planning possibilities exist in choosing the best (host) country to serve as the Trust's situs taking into account such relevant factors as political stability, geographic location, currency fluctuation and the like. And, even though the Trust is established in one country, the assets held by the Trust can be located anywhere in the World. There are numerous countries with laws in effect which make it extremely difficult for United States creditors to reach Trust assets. Generally, these countries also have favorable tax laws. Although these Trusts generally do not receive favorable tax treatment from the Internal Revenue Service (amid increased scrutiny), they more than adequately accomplish their main goal of protecting one's assets from the reach of creditors.

Uniform Transfers to Minors Act

The Uniform Transfers to Minors Act (UTMA) previously replaced the old Uniform Gifts to Minors Act (UGMA), and is now a part of Florida Law. When a bank account is opened or securities are purchased *in trust for* a minor, the Donor has made a completed gift to the minor-Donee. In addition, such property becomes the sole and exclusive property of the minor upon his or her attaining majority.

Under UTMA, a minor is defined as an individual who has not attained twenty-one (21) years of age. (Under UGMA an adult was defined as an individual who has attained the age of eighteen (18)). The increase in age limitation essentially dictates that property held under UTMA generally is not required to be distributed until age twenty-one (21), whereas such property was required to be distributed at age eighteen (18) under UGMA. However, if property is placed in a UTMA account by a Fiduciary (Personal Representative or Trustee) in the absence of a Will, or under a Will or Trust that does not contain an authorization to do so, then the distribution to the minor must be made at age eighteen (18).

Types of Property Held Pursuant to the Act. Under UTMA, virtually any type of property may be subject to transfer to a minor, including real estate, property evidenced by a certificate of title, and future payment pursuant to a contract, such as a promissory note.

UTMA applies to any transfer if, at the time of transfer, the transferor, the minor or the custodian is a resident of the State of Florida, or the custodial property is located in Florida. UTMA further provides that Florida retains jurisdiction in the event of a subsequent change in the residence of the transferor, the minor, the custodian or the removal of custodial property from Florida.

Section 2503(c) Trusts

As an alternative to a gift under the Uniform Transfers to Minors Act, an individual may establish a Section 2503(c) Trust, so named because of the Section of the Internal Revenue Code under which it is authorized. The advantage to this type of Trust is that it qualifies gifts made in Trust for minors for the Annual Gift Tax Exclusion. The general requirements of the Section 2503(c) Trust are as follows:

1. The Trust property and the income therefrom may be expended by, or for the benefit of, the minor-Donee prior to his or her attaining age twenty-one (21). Thus, there can be no real restraint on such expenditures; and

2. To the extent not so expended, Trust property will pass to the Donee upon attaining the age of twenty-one (21), or to the Estate of the Donee if he or she is not then living at age twenty-one (21).

Although the Trust property must be distributable to the beneficiary upon his or her attaining age twenty-one (21), special Trust provisions may permit the beneficiary to extend the term of the Trust until he or she reaches a more mature age, if he or she so chooses. A useful technique is to provide in the Trust that the Trust automatically continues if not terminated by the beneficiary within thirty (30) days of reaching age twenty-one (21).

Annual Exclusion Gifts/Gifts of Tuition and Medical Expenses

As previously discussed, the payment of a minor's tuition and medical expenses, along with Annual Exclusion Gifts, either separately or combined with other Taxable Estate Planning ideas, can decrease the size of the Donor's Estate, while, in effect, passing funds to succeeding generations.

As part of routine Estate Planning, a person should consider naming capable people in advance to handle their affairs in the event of future incapacity. Likewise, parents of minor children should designate substitutes for themselves to raise their children and administer property left to their children in the event of the parent's death or incapacity. In the absence of such advance designations, costly Guardianship proceedings may ensue where a Probate Judge typically appoints an individual, chosen from a field of applicants, to serve as Guardian of the person and property involved. The person selected by the Court may be a total stranger to the affected person's family, its history and circumstances. The better practice is for the reader to carefully consider and name, in advance, the person or persons he or she wants to assume these responsibilities. Although the Court is not *bound* to appoint any designated guardian, if such person is otherwise qualified to serve, he or she is preferable to anyone unfamiliar with the family, its property and dynamics. There are two situations in which advance designations are desirable.

Upon Capacity. In Florida, a competent adult may name a Pre-Need Guardian of the person or property or both in the event of incapacity by Declarant making a written Declaration that names such Guardian to serve in the event of the Declarant's incapacity. The written Declaration must reasonably identify the Declarant and Pre-Need Guardian and be signed by the Declarant in the presence of at least two (2) attesting witnesses who are present at the same time. The Pre-Need Guardian shall assume the duties of guardian upon an adjudication of the Declarant's incapacity. A sample Declaration of Pre-Need Guardian appears as Exhibit XI to this book.

In case of Minority. Similarly, both parents, natural or adoptive, if living, or the surviving parent, may nominate a Pre-Need Guardian of the person or property of both of the parent's minor child by making a written Declaration that names such Guardian to serve if the minor's last surviving parent becomes incapacitated or dies. The written Declaration must reasonably identify the Declarant or Declarants and the designated Pre-Need

Guardian and must be signed by the Declarant or Declarants in the presence of at least two (2) attesting witnesses who are present at the same time. The Pre-Need Guardian shall assume the duties of Guardian immediately upon an adjudication of incapacity of the last surviving parent or the death of the last surviving parent. A sample Declaration of Pre-Need Guardian for Minor appears as Exhibit XII to this book.

Note: A person's selection of an individual to serve as their Pre-Need Guardian by means of a written Declaration may not be honored by a Probate Judge if such named individual exhibits bad behavior, is conflicted, or acts in a manner which is not in the best interest(s) of the Declarant. As with the nomination of a Personal Representative in an Estate, the Court has discretion to refuse to appoint a designated individual who is demonstrated to be unfit to serve due to lack of character, integrity or the like.

DURABLE POWER OF ATTORNEY

Florida permits an individual (the Principal) to execute what is known as a Durable Power of Attorney, authorizing another individual or entity (bank, trust company, etc.) to serve as his or her Attorney-in-Fact (the Agent) to act on their behalf in the handling of some or all of their affairs. Unlike a general power of attorney, a Durable Power of Attorney continues to be effective after the Principal becomes disabled or incapacitated. However, in the event a Petition for the Adjudication of Incapacity is filed in a Court of competent jurisdiction, which questions the capacity of the Principal, all powers under the Durable Power of Attorney are automatically suspended. In appointing a Guardian for the Principal, the Court may authorize the Agent to resume the exercise of some or all the powers. All powers of attorney, regardless of whether they are durable or general powers, terminate at death.

Florida Law regarding the Durable Power of Attorney was substantially amended in October, 2011 to provide greater scope and variety of such powers. The new law allows a Principal to grant authority to an Agent to take significant actions that can impact the Principal's Estate Plan or gifting program. Known as "superpowers," the following powers may be given to an Agent under this provision:

1. Create an inter vivos trust.

2. With respect to a trust created by or on behalf of the Principal, amend, modify, revoke, or terminate the trust, but only if the trust instrument explicitly provides for amendment, modification, revocation, or termination by the Agent.

3. Make a gift of any of the Principal's property outright to or for the benefit of a person, including by the exercise of a presently exercisable general power of appointment held by the Principal, which may or may not be limited to the federal gift tax annual exclusion amount, as specified in the Durable Power of Attorney.

4. Create or change rights of survivorship.

5. Create or change a beneficiary designation.

6. Waive the Principal's right to be a beneficiary of a joint and survivor annuity, including a survivor benefit under a retirement plan.

7. Disclaim property and powers of appointment.

These "superpowers" may only be created by the Principal **initialing** next to the enumerated authority contained in the body of the Durable Power of Attorney Instrument. Otherwise, Agents are now under a mandatory duty to preserve the Principal's Estate Plan. Also, the Durable Power of Attorney must now be executed before two (2) witnesses and be acknowledged before a Notary Public. To come within this amended law, the Durable Power of Attorney document must have been executed on or after October 1, 2011.

Durable Powers of Attorney should contain express authorization enabling its holder to gain access to any and all of the Principal's medical records and related information under the Health Insurance Portability and Accountability Act of 1996 (a/k/a HIPAA).

More so now than ever before, care should be exercised in the choice or selection of an Agent, particularly where superpowers are created by a Principal. Opportunities for abuse by an Agent are necessarily enlarged by the grant of authority to alter title to the Principal's assets, create lifetime/testamentary arrangements which by-pass or supercede existing Estate Planning documents that were previously executed by the Principal. For this reason, the new law has created a process of judicial review under which a Court of competent jurisdiction may construe or enforce a Durable Power of Attorney, review the Agent's conduct, terminate the Agent's authority, remove the Agent, or grant other appropriate relief.

A sample Durable Power of Attorney appears as Exhibit VIII to this book.

HEALTH CARE SURROGATE DESIGNATION

Florida Law allows an individual to designate a Surrogate to make health care decisions on his or her behalf. Such individual is appointed through a "Health Care Surrogate Designation" or "Health Care Power of Attorney."

The Surrogate makes specified health care decisions on behalf of the maker of the document. The following matters are within the scope of the Surrogate's power: the authority to hire and fire medical personnel; consent or withhold consent to conventional and unconventional medical treatment; authorize pain relief medications or rehabilitative programs; change accommodations, including hospital, nursing home or hospice care; and to review all confidential medical or related records and information.

The Health Care Surrogate does not terminate in the event of any physical or mental disability and is exercisable from the date it is created. If properly worded, the Surrogate may now gain access to the individual's health care and medical records notwithstanding the privacy restrictions imposed by the Health Insurance Portability and Accountability Act of 1996 (HIPAA).

A sample Health Care Surrogate Designation appears as Exhibit IX to this book.

The State of Florida recognizes the right of competent persons to direct that their lives not be prolonged by artificial means under certain circumstances. This right is subject to certain interests of society, such as the protection of human life and the preservation of ethical standards in the medical profession. The Legislature found that the artificial prolonging of life for persons (i) with a terminal condition; (ii) with an end-stage condition; or (iii) in a persistent vegetative state may secure only a precarious and burdensome existence while providing nothing medically necessary or beneficial to the patient.

In order that the rights and intentions of persons with such conditions may be respected even after they are no longer able to participate actively in decisions concerning themselves, and to encourage communication between such patients, their families and their physicians, the Legislature declared that the Laws of Florida shall recognize the right of a competent adult to make an oral or written Declaration instructing his or her physician to provide, withhold or withdraw life-prolonging procedures or to designate another to make such treatment decisions, in the event such person is diagnosed as suffering from one of these conditions or is in such a state. Such a Declaration may help to avoid protracted and costly Court battles over the Declarant's intentions and desires in these circumstances.

Any competent adult may make a written Declaration directing the withholding or withdrawal of life-prolonging procedures in the event he or she suffers from:

1. An "end-stage condition" - which is defined in the Florida Statutes as an irreversible condition that is caused by injury, disease, or illness which has resulted in progressively severe and permanent deterioration, and which, to a reasonable degree of medical probability, treatment of the condition would be ineffective.

---

2. A "persistent vegetative state" - which is defined in the Florida Statutes as a permanent and irreversible condition of unconsciousness in which there is:

(a) The absence of voluntary action or cognitive behavior of any kind.

(b) An inability to communicate or interact purposefully with the environment.

3. A "terminal condition" - which is defined in the Florida Statutes as a condition caused by injury, disease, or illness from which there is no reasonable medical probability of recovery and which, without treatment, can be expected to cause death.

The written Declaration must be signed by the Declarant in the presence of two (2) subscribing witnesses, at least one (1) of whom is not a spouse or blood relative of the Declarant. If the Declarant is physically unable to sign the written Declaration, his or her Declaration may be given orally, in which case one of the witnesses must subscribe the Declarant's signature in the Declarant's presence and at his or her direction

It is the responsibility of the Declarant to notify his or her attending physician that a Declaration has been made. If the Declarant is comatose, incapacitated or otherwise medically or physically incapable of providing such notification, any other person may notify the attending physician of the existence of the Declaration.

An attending physician who is notified of the existence of a Declaration must promptly make the written Declaration, or a copy thereof, a part of the Declarant's medical records; or, if an oral Declaration, the attending physician must make such fact a part of the medical records.

The "Right to Die Declaration" or "Living Will" may be revoked in one of the following three (3) ways:

1.   By a writing, dated and signed by the Declarant.   The Statute does not require that the revocation be witnessed.

2.   By the physical cancellation or destruction by either the Declarant or another, in the Declarant's presence and at his or her direction; or

3.   By the Declarant's oral expression of his or her intent to revoke.   The Statute does not indicate to whom the oral expression must be made, although a revocation becomes effective when communicated to the attending physician.   No civil or criminal liability is imposed upon any person for failing to act upon a revocation if that person has actual knowledge of such revocation.

A sample Living Will (Right to Die Declaration) appears as Exhibit X to this book.

Good Estate Planning can help avoid unnecessary conflicts between loved ones upon the death of a family member. However, sometimes good Estate Planning is not enough. This section of the book will discuss common litigation issues and / or problems that may arise after the death of a family member. Estate and Trust litigation can be expensive and often involves issues that are emotional, personal and extremely sensitive to the participating parties. Family dynamics may also serve to fuel such post-mortem controversies.

Some of the most fertile areas for litigation occur when the family member:

- Arranges ownership of various bank and/or brokerage accounts contrary to the terms of his or her testamentary documents.

- Designates beneficiaries of Life Insurance Policies, Retirement Plans and/or Annuities that are inconsistent with the terms of other such assets or his or her testamentary documents.

- Fails to specify which of his or her heirs should pay the expenses of administrating their Estate or how to allocate the tax liabilities.

- Fails to provide their direction if an heir or beneficiary fails to survive them or dies simultaneously with them.

- Fails to provide for remarriage of an intended heir or beneficiary.

- Fails to provide the proper protection for a problem child, a dependent spouse, a spendthrift sister, a needy parent, etc.

- Arranges ownership of real estate in a way that by-passes or is inconsistent with the planned disposition provided in his or her testamentary documents.

- Fails to nominate desired Fiduciaries or delineate Fiduciary compensation.

These acts may operate so as to (i) defeat the intentions of the individual as expressed in the Estate Plan (ii) result in the payment of additional/unnecessary Estate Taxes; (iii) cause the failure of bequests to family members and (iv) increase the likelihood of Will contests.

Will and Trust Contests

Litigation attacking the validity of testamentary documents is commonly referred to as Will and Trust contests. Common grounds for a Will and Trust contest include improper execution of the Testamentary Document, incapacity of the person executing the Testamentary Document, fraud, duress, undue influence or mistake.

Proper Execution. When the proper execution of a Will and / or Trust is challenged, the complaint will consist of allegations that the required formalities of execution of the Testamentary Documents were not followed. The litigation will consist of specific and detailed examination of the witnesses, the attorney(s), the notary and anyone else involved in the execution of the document.

In order for a Will to be valid, the Testator must be at least eighteen (18) years of age or an emancipated minor at the time the Will is executed. The Will must be executed in accordance with the statutory formalities required under Florida Law. The Will must be in writing, and signed by the Testator at the end of the document. The Testator must sign in the presence of at least two (2) witnesses or acknowledge his or her signature to at least two (2) witnesses. The witnesses must be competent and sign the Will in the presence of each other **and** the Testator. In Florida, witnesses may be beneficiaries of the Will.

The testamentary aspects of a Trust are invalid unless the instrument is executed by the Settlor (Creator of the Trust) with the formalities of a Will discussed above. Further, if the testamentary plan consists of a "pour over" Will and a Revocable (Living) Trust, the Trust must be executed before the "pour over" Will is executed to be a valid beneficiary of the Estate.

If the challenging party can prove that any of the foregoing formalities were not followed, the Will and / or Trust will be declared invalid.

Fraud, Duress, Undue Influence or Mistake. A Will or Trust is supposed to reflect the testamentary intentions of the Settlor / Testator. If a Will or Trust is procured by fraud, duress, undue influence or mistake, the testamentary intentions of the Testator / Settlor are defeated. As a result, any Will or Trust proven to be procured by fraud, duress, undue influence or mistake will be voided.

A Will or Trust procured by fraud defeats the Testator's / Settlor's testamentary intentions through deceit. The challenging party must show that the perpetrator made fraudulent representations of material facts to the Testator / Settlor with the intent that the fraudulent representations be acted upon which resulted in a Will or Trust that does not express the Testator's / Settlor's true testamentary intentions.

A Will or Trust procured while the Testator or Settlor was under duress may not reflect the testamentary intentions of the Testator or Settlor. To void a Will executed under duress, the challenging party must show that the Will or Trust was created under threat of force or blackmail which served to defeat the Testator's / Settlor's testamentary intentions.

Undue influence is a common challenge to a Will or Trust. It is not uncommon for over zealous heirs to improperly impose their wills and desires on older family members which may result in a Will or Trust which reflects the heir's desires and not the testamentary intentions of the Testator / Settlor.

An important consideration in proving undue influence is the establishment of a *presumption* of undue influence. If a person challenging the Will or Trust is able to make a preliminary showing that one having a substantial benefit under the Will (i.e., a beneficiary) possessed a confidential relationship with the decedent and was active in the procurement of the Will (i.e., recommended attorney or presence at execution), a presumption of undue influence will arise.

Florida Law provides that the presumption of undue influence shifts the burden of proof from the person challenging the Will to the proponent of the Will. Thus, the Will may be voided if the proponent is unable to overcome the presumption.

A Will or Trust challenge based upon mistake requires a showing that the decedent mistakenly executed the wrong document. Mistakes in fact, wording or scriveners errors will not result in the Will or Trust being declared void.

Will and Trust Construction

Sometimes the rights of interested parties as set forth in the Will or Trust are not clear thus requiring a judicial proceeding to construe the Testamentary Document. Litigation to construe the Will or Trust may result from poor planning, facts not considered when drafting the Will or Trust, or changes in circumstances that did not exist or may not have been considered when the Will or Trust was drafted.

When construing the language in a Will or Trust, the intent of the Testator / Settlor is paramount. However, there are some rules of construction which have been codified by state law and/or prior case precedents. A good Estate Planning attorney is aware of these rules of construction and can draft a document to avoid the consequences of these laws/cases if the provisions of the law or prior cases are contrary to the intentions of the Settlor / Testator.

An example of such a codified rule of construction is the antilapse statute which provides that a bequest to a grandparent or lineal descendant of a grandparent (uncle, aunt, mother father, brother, sister etc.) of the Testator who predeceases the Testator will not fail or lapse. Rather, the descendants of the deceased beneficiary will receive the bequest. If the Testator / Settlor does not want the descendants of a beneficiary covered by the antilapse statute to inherit if the beneficiary predeceases the Settlor / Testator, the Will or Trust can specifically provide that the bequest lapses upon the prior death of the beneficiary and the language of the Will or Trust will control.

In Florida, a provision in a Will or Trust purporting to penalize any interested person for contesting the Will or Trust or instituting other proceedings relating to the Estate or Trust is unenforceable.

Accounting Litigation

Trustees and Personal Representatives are required to file Fiduciary Accountings in Florida and serve such Accountings on interested persons in the Estate and Trust. The purpose of the Accounting is to report to the beneficiaries and other interested parties the financial details of the administration of the Trust and Estate.

A Personal Representative of an Estate is required to file an Accounting upon removal, resignation or completion of Estate administration. A Personal Representative may also elect to file an interim Accounting at any time. The Accounting is required to show the assets on hand at the beginning of the Accounting period, all capital transactions of the Estate, all Estate receipts, all Estate disbursements, all Estate distributions to beneficiaries, and the assets on hand at the end of the Accounting period. The Accounting is required to be served on interested persons (beneficiaries, creditors, etc.).

If an interested person does not agree with a transaction reported in the Accounting or believes that the Fiduciary has acted improperly, the interested person can file an Objection to the Accounting. Objections to an interim Accounting and a final

Accounting of a Personal Representative must be filed within thirty (30) days of service or shall be deemed abandoned. When an Objection is filed to a final Accounting, the person filing the Objection must serve a notice of hearing within ninety (90) days of filing the Objection or the Objection will be deemed to be abandoned.

Trustees are required to serve similar Accountings to each qualified beneficiary on an annual basis and upon termination of the Trust or change of Trustee. A qualified beneficiary is defined as beneficiaries currently entitled to Trust income or principal, beneficiaries who would be entitled to distributions if the interests of the current beneficiaries terminated on the date that the Accounting is filed, or beneficiaries who would be entitled to distributions if the Trust terminated in accordance with its terms on the date the Accounting is filed.

A qualified beneficiary is required to bring an action against the Trustee within six (6) months after receipt of a Trust Accounting or a Trust disclosure document which contains a limitation notice (a notification that all actions against the Trustee for breach of trust must be commenced within six (6) months after receipt of the Trust disclosure document) with respect to all matters which are adequately disclosed in the Accounting. A beneficiary who fails to bring an action against the Trustee for a breach of trust disclosed in the Trust Accounting within six (6) months of receipt of the Accounting will be forever barred from bringing the action.

Prudent Investor Rule

Both Trustees and Personal Representatives in Florida are required to invest Trust and Estate assets in accordance with the Prudent Investor Rule which takes into account modern portfolio theories of investing.

The Prudent Investor Rule (the "Rule") requires the Fiduciary to minimize investment risk through portfolio diversification. A properly diversified portfolio leaves only market risk, which, at the proper level, allows growth at a rate meaningfully greater than inflation. A decision to not incur any market risk is not permitted under the Rule because it is a decision to ignore inflation. The Rule also provides that a Fiduciary's duty to make property productive will include securing a return to the principal as well as income production, with these competing interests being balanced in a way that is appropriate to the particular Trust or Estate.

The Rule allows a Fiduciary to delegate decision-making responsibilities and may even require a Fiduciary to seek assistance where the Fiduciary does not have the skills to maintain a properly diversified portfolio. Thus, Fiduciaries who are not sophisticated investors are required to seek professional advice on how to invest the assets of the Estate in a way that satisfies the new Prudent Investor Rule requirements or be subject to possible liability.

If an interested person files an action criticizing the investment decisions of a Fiduciary, the Court will look to the Fiduciary's conduct at the time the investment decision is made to determine if a breach of Fiduciary duty has occurred. In determining the amount of liability for improperly invested accounts, the Rule compares the performance of the portfolio in question to how it would have performed if it had been appropriately invested. Thus, it is important that the Fiduciary obtain appropriate advice to ensure that the assets are invested in accordance with the Prudent Investor Rule.

Creditor Claims

One of the most important duties of a Personal Representative is to ascertain what debts and claims are to be paid by the Estate. Valid claims against the Estate and Trust must be paid before the assets of the Estate and Trust can be distributed to the beneficiaries. To expedite the settlement of the Decedent's Estate, the Probate Code (in Florida) provides a very specific procedure for the notification of creditors and potential claimants, for the filing of claims against the Estate, and for objecting to claims that are not believed to be valid. The procedures set forth for filing claims and the claims themselves are often a source of litigation in Probate.

The Probate Code requires that a Notice to Creditors be published once a week for two (2) consecutive weeks in a newspaper published in the county where the Estate is being administered. All reasonable ascertainable creditors of the Decedent's Estate are required to be served with a Notice to Creditors. The Notice to Creditors contains the name of the Decedent, the file number of the Estate, the address of the Court, the name and address of the Personal Representative and attorney, the date of the publication, and a notification that creditors must file timely claims against the Estate with the Court or be forever barred. If a claim against the Decedent's Estate is not filed within three (3) months after publication of the Notice to Creditors, or within thirty (30) days after the date of service of the Notice to Creditors on a reasonably ascertainable creditor, the claim is forever barred. A Court may extend the time to file a claim only if the claimant can prove that the failure to file a timely claim was the result of fraud, estoppel or insufficient notice of the claims period.

Absolutely no claim can be filed against the Estate more than two (2) years after the Decedent's death regardless of whether the foregoing claim procedures are followed.

Examples of claims that are required to be timely filed or be forever barred include any agreement with the Decedent which is intended to be enforced against the Estate (such as nuptial agreements, real estate sale contracts, buy-sell agreements, etc.), last illness expenses, lawsuits against the Decedent (both pending and potential lawsuits), outstanding credit card debts, claims for alimony and support, and funeral expenses.

The Personal Representative or any interested person in the Estate may object to a claim by filing a written Objection within four (4) months of the first publication of Notice to Creditors or within thirty (30) days after the timely filing of a claim, whichever occurs later. If no Objection is filed, the claim must be paid. If an Objection is filed, the claimant has thirty (30) days after being served with an Objection to file an independent action to establish the validity of the claim. Failure to file an independent action within the thirty (30) day period will result in the claim being barred. If an independent action is timely filed by the claimant, the interested parties will litigate the validity of the claim.

All valid claims are required to be paid within one (1) year from the date of the first publication of the Notice to Creditors.

Challenging the Appointment of Individuals Designated to Serve in Fiduciary Positions

As discussed elsewhere in this book, a person may designate a spouse, child or trusted friend or advisor to serve in one or more Fiduciary positions, such as Personal Representative of their Estate, Trustee of a Trust, or holder of their Durable Power of Attorney, designated Health Care Surrogate or designated Pre-Need Guardian. However, just because a person (or corporation) is named in one or more of these capacities in an otherwise valid, legal document **does not guarantee** his or her appointment or service as such. There is no absolute legal right to serve in such designated capacities. A Court of competent jurisdiction always has the authority to refuse to appoint such designated person to any Fiduciary position if it can be demonstrated that such individual is unfit to hold such office or position. Typical grounds for disqualification include mental or physical incapacity which renders such person incapable of performing their duties; holding or acquiring conflicting or adverse interests against the Estate or Trust that will or may interfere with its administration; or demonstrated acts of bad behavior or moral turpitude that call into question the character, integrity or honesty of the designated Fiduciary. Mere hostility or ill-will is not a sufficient basis to disqualify an otherwise eligible individual who has been designated by a Testator, Settlor, Principal or Power Holder in a properly executed, legal document to serve in a Fiduciary capacity.

The proper legal vehicle to use in challenging the appointment of a Fiduciary is a Petition filed with the Court requesting that the nominated person's fitness to serve in such capacity be formally determined. Every Court has the discretion to examine the character, integrity and honesty of those seeking to serve in Fiduciary positions. This is true because a Fiduciary is a person or corporation which is appointed to a special position of trust and confidence and who owes Fiduciary duties to all he or she serves or represents. For example, it has often been said that a Fiduciary owes a duty of undivided loyalty and a duty to refrain from self-dealing. Before conferring this special power and authority on anyone – even someone designated to serve as such – a Court must review his or her qualifications, credentials and experience, and, where such examination supports the conclusion that the designated person lacks the necessary qualities and characteristics to properly discharge his or her duties, the Court may legitimately refuse to allow him or her to serve because, once appointed to such position, he or she may use the resources of the Estate or Trust to defend himself/herself against removal from office. Therefore, no Court should ever appoint a known or suspected unfit person to a Fiduciary position lest it be accused of acting irresponsibly.

Summary of Estate and Trust Litigation

As can be seen, there are many areas of potential disagreement and litigation after the death of a loved one. Although some situations and family dynamics make post-mortem litigation inevitable, anticipation of potential disagreements and litigation – coupled with good Estate Planning advice – may help avoid or lessen the risk or likelihood of such litigation and result in substantial savings to the Estate or Trust. Thus, a well conceived Estate Plan does not only operate to reduce taxes, but can preserve and promote family harmony. One thing is certain: when the Testator dies, the "glue" is gone and years of frustrations and hard feelings among family members may erupt into expensive and protracted litigation. Failing to address these important issues in the Estate Plan may result in the lawyers becoming the majority beneficiaries of the Estate or Trust and not the family members.

According to recent statistics, Florida has over three million senior citizens residing within its borders. Inevitably, some of these individuals will lose their capacity to handle their personal and/or financial affairs each and every day.

In anticipation of this, Florida has adopted a comprehensive Court-supervised process of determining when and how its residents are entitled to the protection of its Courts through a system of both voluntary and involuntary Guardianship laws.

Voluntary Guardianships

A competent individual (Petitioner) may designate another to serve as Guardian of his or her person and/or property at any time. Such appointment is authorized by law provided that a licensed physician furnishes a certificate stating that he or she has examined the Petitioner and that such individual is competent to understand the nature of the Guardianship and the delegation of authority associated therewith. One major drawback of the voluntary Guardianship is that it may be terminated at any time by the Petitioner – assuming his or her continued capacity. The voluntary Guardianship is different from a Pre-Need Guardian Designation which is discussed elsewhere in this book.

Involuntary Guardianships

Involuntary Guardianships, as the name implies, involve a formal adjudication of incapacity by a Court of law after notice to all interested persons.

The process begins with the filing of a verified Petition to determine the incapacity of a resident of this state, together with a Petition for the appointment of a Guardian for such incapacitated person which must be filed at the same time. The Court then appoints an Examining Committee consisting of three (3) members who shall each examine the alleged incapacitated person and file a written report listing their findings, on the basis of which a Hearing is then held at which such person's capacity shall be formally determined. Due process requires that the alleged incapacitated person be represented by counsel and that he or she be further entitled to be present at such adjudication Hearing.

At least one of the three (3) members of the Examining Committee must be a psychiatrist or other physician. The remaining members must be either a psychologist, gerontologist, another psychiatrist or other physician, a registered nurse, nurse practitioner, licensed social worker, a person with an advanced degree in gerontology from an accredited institution of higher education, or other person who by knowledge, skill, experience, training, or education may, in the Court's discretion, advise the Court in the form of an expert opinion. At least one (1) of the three (3) members of the Examining Committee must have knowledge of the type of incapacity alleged in the Petition. If the alleged incapacitated person's attending or family physician is available for consultation, the Examining Committee must consult with the physician.

If a majority of the Examining Committee members conclude that the alleged incapacitated person is not incapacitated in any respect, the Court must dismiss the Petition.

If the Court determines that the person (Ward) is incapacitated, it must decide what type of Guardian is appropriate to be appointed for the Ward's person or property or both.

A Plenary Guardian is a person who has been approved by the Court to exercise all delegable legal rights and powers of the Ward after the Court has found that the Ward lacks the capacity to perform all of the tasks necessary to care for his or her person and/or property.

A Limited Guardian is a person who has been appointed by the Court to exercise only the legal rights and powers specifically designated by Court Order entered after the Court has found that the Ward lacks capacity to do some, but not all, of the tasks necessary to care for his or her person and/or property.

In terms of persons who may serve as a Guardian, any resident of this state who is sui juris and is eighteen (18) years of age or older may serve as Guardian of a resident Ward.

A non-resident of this state may serve as Guardian of a resident Ward if he or she is related by lineal consanguinity to the Ward; a legally adopted child or adoptive parent of the Ward; a spouse, brother, sister, uncle, aunt, niece, or nephew of the Ward or someone related by lineal consanguinity to any such person; or the spouse of a person otherwise qualified.

Qualified banks or trust companies may serve as Guardians of property only. Certain persons may be disqualified from serving as Guardians by virtue of adverse interests or conflicts of interest, illness or incapacity, unsuitability, or conviction of a felony. When family members are in conflict over who should serve as Guardian, the Court may appoint a neutral, independent Professional Guardian to act in such capacity. A Professional Guardian is a person who has the care of three (3) or more Wards and must be registered with and overseen by the Statewide Public Guardianship Office in the Florida Department of Elder Affairs.

Guardianship Proceedings

Once appointed, a Guardian is required to file annual plans, reports and accountings with the Court, and most actions of the Guardian require Court supervision and advance approval, which operate to provide continuing protection of the Ward and his or her property throughout the Guardianship process.

Emergency Temporary Guardianship

A Court, prior to appointment of a Guardian but after a Petition for Determination of Incapacity has been filed, may appoint an Emergency Temporary Guardian for the person or property or both of an alleged incapacitated person where the Court specifically finds that there appears to be imminent danger that the physical or mental health or safety of the person will be seriously impaired or that the person's property is in danger of being wasted, misappropriated or lost unless immediate action is taken.

When to Initiate Guardianship Proceedings

Situations that develop within families which lend themselves to the establishment of protective Guardianships may include the following:

- Patriarch develops Alzheimer's, dementia or a similar memory-loss disease, and his wife/children move in on his life savings.

- Local siblings unduly influence a parent to re-write his or her Will to exclude distant siblings and descendants.

- Spouse misuses a Durable Power of Attorney to transfer the incapacitated spouse's interest in the couple's home to himself or herself and some but not all descendants.

- Spouse makes unauthorized transfers of the incapacitated spouse's assets to himself or herself and/or favored family members.

- Child misuses a Durable Power of Attorney to change the beneficiaries of a parent's life insurance policy to that child or that child's family to the exclusion of other children.

- Child takes incapacitated parent's credit card and makes unauthorized charges of thousands of dollars.

- Neighbor intercepts incapacitated person's mail and misappropriates pension checks.

- Mentally incapacitated parent receives dozens of mail solicitations each week and writes checks in response to many of the solicitations before a child can intercede.

- Incapacitated relative buries money in the ground surrounding his or her home because he or she distrusts banks and/or fears government intrusion into his or her affairs.

- Sibling convinces his or her parents to transfer title to the parents' home to them to avoid probate and save taxes, to the exclusion of other sibling(s).

Termination of Guardianship

In the event that a Ward regains his or her ability to exercise some or all of their rights which were previously removed at the initiation of the Guardianship and the same is confirmed through a current medical examination, the Court may restore all or some of such rights going forward. If full capacity is restored, the Guardianship is terminated, and the Guardian is discharged. The Ward's death also terminates the Guardianship. Assets of the Guardianship will, upon the Ward's death, be added to the Ward's Probate Estate and will pass under the Ward's Last Will and Testament or by Intestacy if no valid Will exists.

Estate Planning is an evolving process, shaped by Legislation, Internal Revenue Service Regulations and Court Rulings.

In the past ten (10) years, numerous changes have been made or proposed with respect to Estate Taxes, including abolishment of the Estate Tax, the surcharge of larger Estates, and elimination of the Unified Credit. State laws have changed also regarding the phase-out of state death tax credits and decoupling from the Federal Estate Tax system.

The Economic Growth and Tax Relief Reconciliation Act of 2001, signed into law (in June 2001) by President George W. Bush, increased the Unified Credit so that by the year 2009, every taxpayer may transfer assets during their lifetime as gifts and at death as part of their Estate valued in the aggregate at three million five hundred thousand dollars ($3,500,000), free from Estate and Gift Taxes. Effective in December 2010, the Tax Relief, Unemployment Insurance Reauthorization, and Job Creation Act of 2010 became law for two (2) years (2011 and 2012) and provided for a reduction in the Federal Estate Tax rate from forty-five percent (45%) to thirty-five percent (35%) and an increase in the Exemption Equivalent from three million five hundred thousand dollars ($3,500,000) to five million dollars ($5,000,000). And, as stated previously, the Gift Tax Exemption will be the same as the Federal Estate Tax Exemption (five million dollars ($5,000,000)) in 2011 and 2012.

It is important to understand that this Act is currently scheduled to "sunset" on December 31, 2012, meaning that all provisions of the Law do not apply for taxable years beginning after December 31, 2012. Thereafter, the Federal Estate Tax is slated to revert to the 2001 level with an Exemption of one million dollars ($1,000,000) per individual and a top rate of fifty-five percent (55%).

The reader should note that the Estate Planning concepts contained in this book have valid purposes regardless of changes in Estate Tax rates, the Unified Credit Exemption, or other changes which have been, or are currently being, considered.

The concepts and techniques embodied in this book should be viewed in this perspective, and implemented only in consultation with appropriate professional advisors based on Regulations, Exemptions and rates then in effect.

LIST OF EXHIBITS

DECLARATION OF NON-DOMICILE

This is my Declaration of Non-Domicile that I am filing in the State of New York this day upon advice of counsel.

I, TOM TAXPAYER, formerly of City of Stress, Taxable County, New York, hereby certify that I have abandoned my domicile and residency in New York to become a bona fide resident of the State of Florida.

I now reside at 1 Sunshine Way, City of Paradise, County of Palm Beach, Florida, and have resided there since January 1, 2001, and intend for the State of Florida to be my legal domicile.

I further certify that I have complied with all requirements of legal residence of the State of Florida. Attached hereto as composite Exhibit "A" is a true and correct copy of my Declaration of Domicile filed in Palm Beach County, Florida, on January 1, 2001.

Under penalties of perjury, I have executed this document this _____ day of _____, 20___.

Signed, Sealed and Delivered
in the presence of:

SAMPLE

_____   _____
                               TOM TAXPAYER

_____

SWORN TO and subscribed before me this _____ day of _____, 20___.

(SEAL)   _____
                               Notary Public
                               State of Florida
                               My commission expires:

Exhibit I

DECLARATION OF DOMICILE

This is my Declaration of Domicile in the State of Florida that I am filing this day in accordance and in conformity with Section 222.17, Florida Statutes Annotated.

I, TOM TAXPAYER, became a bona fide resident of the State of Florida on January 1, 2001, and I reside in and maintain an abode at 1 Sunshine Way, City of Paradise, County of Palm Beach, Florida, which I recognize and intend to maintain as my permanent home.

My former residence was in the City of Stress, Taxable County, State of New York.

I further certify that I have complied with all requirements of a legal resident of this State. I understand the penalty for perjury is up to 5 years in State Prison (Section 837.02, Florida Statutes Annotated).

Signed, Sealed and Delivered
in the presence of:

SAMPLE

_____   _____
                                            TOM TAXPAYER

_____

SWORN TO and subscribed before me this _____ day of _____, 20___.

(SEAL)   _____
                               Notary Public
                               State of Florida
                               My commission expires:

Exhibit II

SPECIAL DECLARATION OF DOMICILE
FOR INDIVIDUAL MAINTAINING PLACE(S) OF ABODE IN OTHER STATE(S)

Pursuant to and in conformity with Sections 222.17(2) & 3, Florida Statutes, Annotated, this is my sworn statement evidencing Florida Domicile.

I, TOM TAXPAYER, became a bona fide resident of the State of Florida on January 1, 2001, and I reside in and maintain an abode at 1 Sunshine Way, City of Paradise, Palm Beach County, Florida, which I recognize and intend to maintain as my predominant and principal home.

My former legal residence was City of Stress, Taxable County, State of New York, and I maintain another place of abode at 1040 High Tax Lane, Stress, New York, which I acknowledge is not my predominant and principal home. I further acknowledge that I have abandoned my former legal domicile in the State of New York as of the date referred to above and have no intention to return there.

I further certify that I will comply with all requirements of a legal resident of this State.

Under penalties of perjury, I have executed this document this _____ day of _____, 20___.

Signed, Sealed and Delivered
in the presence of:

SAMPLE

_____

_____
TOM TAXPAYER

SWORN TO and subscribed before me this _____ day of _____, 20___.

(SEAL)

_____
Notary Public
State of Florida
My commission expires:

Exhibit III

TABLE OF SELECTED
STATE INHERITANCE/ESTATE TAX RATES

State	Spouse	Others
Connecticut	None	7.2% - 12%
Delaware	Up to 16%	Up to 16%
FLORIDA	**None**	**None**
Indiana	None	1% - 20%
Iowa	None	5% - 15%
Kentucky	None	4% - 16%
Louisiana	2% - 3%	2% - 10%
Maryland	None	Up to 10%
Massachusetts	None	Up to 16%
New Hampshire	None	18%
New York	None	Up to 16%
North Carolina	Up to 16%	Up to 16%
Ohio	None	Up to 7%
Pennsylvania	None	4.5% - 15%
Tennessee	None	5.5% - 9.5%

OTHER STATES WITHOUT
INHERITANCE/ESTATE TAXES:

Alabama, Alaska, Arizona, Arkansas, California, Colorado, District of Columbia, Georgia, Illinois, Michigan, Mississippi, Missouri, Montana, Nevada, New Mexico, North Dakota, South Carolina, Utah, Virginia, West Virginia and Wisconsin.

(Note that some or all of these states do levy an Inheritance/Estate Tax, however, the state tax is tied to the Federal Credit for State Death Taxes which was phased out after December 31, 2004 and scheduled to return beginning January 1, 2013.)

Exhibit IV

CHART OF INTESTATE SUCCESSION
UNDER FLORIDA LAW
(DYING WITHOUT A WILL)

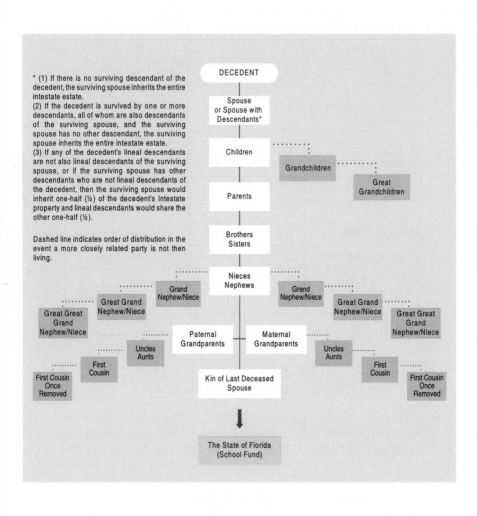

* (1) If there is no surviving descendant of the decedent, the surviving spouse inherits the entire intestate estate.

(2) If the decedent is survived by one or more descendants, all of whom are also descendants of the surviving spouse, and the surviving spouse has no other descendant, the surviving spouse inherits the entire intestate estate.

(3) If any of the decedent's lineal descendants are not also lineal descendants of the surviving spouse, or if the surviving spouse has other descendants who are not lineal descendants of the decedent, then the surviving spouse would inherit one-half (½) of the decedent's Intestate property and lineal descendants would share the other one-half (½).

Dashed line indicates order of distribution in the event a more closely related party is not then living.

DECEDENT

Spouse
or Spouse with
Descendants*

Children

Grandchildren

Great
Grandchildren

Parents

Brothers
Sisters

Nieces
Nephews

Grand
Nephew/Niece

Grand
Nephew/Niece

Great Grand
Nephew/Niece

Great Grand
Nephew/Niece

Great Great
Grand
Nephew/Niece

Great Great
Grand
Nephew/Niece

Paternal
Grandparents

Maternal
Grandparents

Uncles
Aunts

Uncles
Aunts

First
Cousin

First
Cousin

First Cousin
Once
Removed

First Cousin
Once
Removed

Kin of Last Deceased
Spouse

The State of Florida
(School Fund)

Exhibit V

CHART OF LEGAL BLOOD RELATIONS
(CONSANGUINITY)

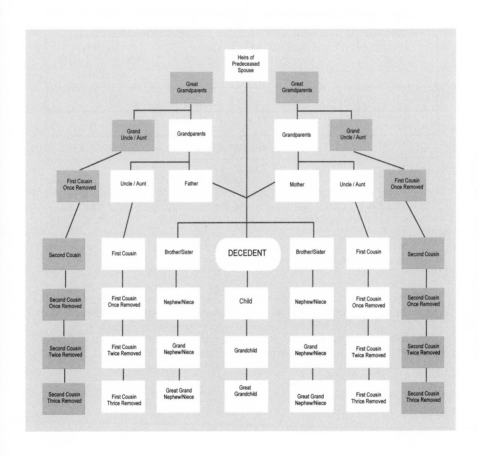

Exhibit VI

TABLE OF UNIFIED
FEDERAL ESTATE AND GIFT TAX RATES [1,2]

Based upon the new Tax Relief, Unemployment Insurance Reauthorization, and Job Creation Act of 2010, from 2011 through 2013 the Estate and Gift Tax Rates and Unified Credit effective exemption for Estate Tax purposes are as shown in the Table below:

Calendar Year	Estate and GST Tax death-time transfer exemption	Highest Estate and Gift Tax Rates [3]
2011	$5 million	35%
2012	$5.12 million	35%
2013	$1 million	55%

[1.] Lifetime gifts within the Annual Exclusion Amount ($13,000 per donee, per year) are not taxable gifts and do not reduce the Unified Credit. Lifetime gifts which exceed the Annual Exclusion reduce the Unified Credit otherwise available to offset Estate Taxes upon death.

[2.] The Federal Estate Tax is reduced by the Unified Credit Exemption Amount applicable in the year of death.

[3.] Under the Economic Growth and Tax Relief Reconciliation Act of 2001, the Estate Tax was repealed for 2010, with the 2001 exemption amount and tax rates applicable for decedent's dying after December 31, 2010. The Tax Relief, Unemployment Insurance Reauthorization, and Job Creation Act of 2010 extended the return of the 2001 exemption amount and tax rates until January 1, 2013.

Exhibit VII

DURABLE POWER OF ATTORNEY

BY THIS DURABLE POWER OF ATTORNEY I, TOM TAXPAYER, residing in the City of Paradise, Palm Beach County, Florida, hereby appoint _____ as my Agent to manage my affairs, in accordance with Part II of Chapter 709, Florida Statutes Annotated.

Revocation of All Prior Durable Power(s) of Attorney. The execution of this Durable Power of Attorney shall revoke any/all Powers of Attorney previously executed by me in this State or in any other State or jurisdiction.

Durable Power. This Durable Power of Attorney shall not be affected by any physical or mental incapacity that I may suffer subsequent to the date of execution of this Instrument except as provided by statute, and shall be exercisable from and after this date. All acts done by my designated Agent pursuant to this Power shall bind me, my heirs, devisees and the Personal Representative(s) of my estate. This Durable Power of Attorney is and shall be non-delegable.

Multiple Agents. If more than one person is serving as my Agent, all powers conferred upon such Agent shall be exercisable by each of my Agent acting alone, without the approval or consent of any of my other Agent named herein.

Duration of Power. My Agent may exercise the authority granted under this Durable Power of Attorney until such time as I die, revoke the power, or am adjudicated totally or partially incapacitated by a court of competent jurisdiction, except as may be otherwise determined by such court.

Suspension of Power of Attorney. If any person initiates judicial proceedings to determine my incapacity or for the appointment of a guardian advocate, the authority granted under the Power of Attorney is suspended until the petition is dismissed or withdrawn, or the court enters an order authorizing my Attorney-in-Fact to exercise one or more powers granted under this Power of Attorney.

If an emergency arises after initiation of proceedings to determine incapacity and before adjudication regarding my capacity, my Attorney-in-Fact may petition the court in which the proceeding is pending for authorization to exercise a power granted under this Power of Attorney. The petition must set forth the nature of the emergency, the property or matter involved, and the power to be exercised by my Attorney-in-Fact.

Revocation of this Power of Attorney. I may revoke this Power of Attorney by expressing the revocation in a subsequently-executed Power of Attorney or other writing signed by me, notice of which I may give to my Attorney-in-Fact selected hereunder.

Exhibit VIII

Property Subject to Durable Power of Attorney. This Durable Power of Attorney applies to any and all interests in property which I may own, including, without limitation, all of my interests in real property, including homestead real property; all of my personal property, tangible or intangible; all property held in any type of joint tenancy, including a tenancy in common, joint tenancy with right of survivorship, or a tenancy by the entirety; all property over which I hold a general, limited or special power of appointment; choses in action; and all other contractual or statutory rights or elections, including, but not limited to, any and all rights and/or elections in any probate or similar proceeding to which I am now or may in the future become entitled.

Powers of Agent. Without limiting the broad powers conferred by the preceding provisions, I hereby authorize my Agent to:

1. Collect all sums of money and other property that may be payable or belonging to me, and to execute receipts, releases, cancellations or discharges.

2. Settle any account in which I have an interest and to pay or receive the balance of that account as the case may require.

3. Enter any safe deposit box or other place of safekeeping standing in my name alone or jointly with another and to remove the contents and to make additions, substitutions and replacements.

4. Borrow money on such terms and with such security as my Agent may think fit and to execute all notes, mortgages and other Instruments that my Agent finds necessary or desirable.

5. Draw, accept, endorse or otherwise deal with any checks or other commercial or mercantile instruments, specifically including the right to purchase, sell or make changes to or withdrawals from any savings account, certificate of deposit, money market account or the like.

6. Execute stock powers or similar documents on my behalf and delegate to a transfer agent or similar person the authority to register any stocks, bonds or other securities, either into or out of my or my nominee's name.

7. Redeem bonds issued by the United States Government or any of its agencies, subdivisions, municipalities and any other bonds and any certificates of deposit or other similar assets belonging to me.

8. Sell bonds, shares of stock, warrants, debentures, or any other assets belonging to me, and execute all deeds, bills of sale, assignments and other instruments necessary or proper to evidence or effectuate their transfer to the purchaser or purchasers, and give good receipts and discharges for all money payable in respect to them.

Exhibit VIII

9. Invest any and all of my property and/or the proceeds thereof as well as the proceeds of any redemptions or sales and any other of my money, in bonds, shares of stock or other securities, partnerships, joint ventures and business enterprises as my Agent shall think fit.

10. Vote and exercise all rights and options, including stock options, and execute all required consents in respect to any of my property.

11. Vote at all meetings of stockholders of any company and otherwise act as my Agent or proxy in respect of my shares of stock or other securities or investments that now or hereafter belong to me, and appoint substitutes or proxies with respect to any of those shares of stock.

12. Execute on my behalf any and all tax returns (Federal, state and local) and act for me in any examination, audit, hearing, conference or litigation relating to taxes, including authority to file and prosecute refund claims and enter into any settlements.

13. Sell, rent, lease for any term, transfer, convey, exchange or mortgage any real estate or interests in it, including homestead property, for such considerations and upon such terms and conditions as my Agent may deem fit, and execute, acknowledge and deliver all instruments conveying or encumbering title to property owned by me alone as well as any owned by me as a tenant by the entireties, tenant in common, joint tenant with right of survivorship, or otherwise. If I am married, my Agent may not mortgage, convey or otherwise encumber homestead property without joinder of my spouse, my spouse's legal guardian, or my spouse's Agent.

14. Retain counsel and prosecute, defend and settle all actions or other legal proceedings relating to my property and/or any asset of my estate or any part of it or relating to any matter in which I may be concerned in any way.

15. Purchase bonds issued by the United States that can be applied at face or maturity value on account of Federal Estate Tax liabilities, commonly known as "Flower Bonds."

16. Hire accountants, attorneys-at-law, clerks, workmen and others, and to remove them, and to appoint others in their place, and to pay and allow to the persons to be employed such salaries, wages or other remunerations as my said Agent shall think fit.

17. Do anything regarding my estate, property and affairs that I could do myself, which shall include all authority contained in Section 709.2201, Florida Statutes Annotated, as the same now exists and as it may be amended or revised but shall only include the authority contained in Section 709.2202 to the extent it is set forth herein. This authorization includes, and is not limited to, requesting the release of any and all information governed by the

Exhibit VIII

Health Insurance Portability and Accountability Act of 1996 (a/k/a HIPAA), 42 USC 130 2d and 45 CFR 160-164.

18. Transfer any real or personal property to the then-acting Trustee(s) of any existing or future Trust Agreement or Declaration of Trust of which I am a Settlor or Grantor, and to make transfers or withdrawals of any or all monies, real or personal property constituting the Trust Estate thereof, in accordance with the terms of such Trust Instrument.

19. Conduct banking transactions as provided in Section 709.2208(1), Florida Statutes Annotated.

20. Conduct investment transactions as provided in Section 709.2208(2), Florida Statutes Annotated.

Superpowers of Agents. If my initials do not appear next to the specific enumerated authority provided below in this Section, my Agent does not have the power to exercise the authority provided therein. My Agent may exercise the following enumerated powers if my initial is next to the specific enumeration of authority granted therein to the extent necessary to preserve my estate plan, to the extent actually known by my Agent, if preserving the estate plan is consistent with my best interest based on all relevant factors set forth in 709.2114(4) Florida Statutes Annotated:

1. Disclaim property and powers of appointment without Court approval in like manner as a Guardian may execute the same pursuant to the standards and provisions set forth in Sections 689.21 and/or 732.801, Florida Statutes Annotated, (or provided by Section 2518 of the Internal Revenue Code of 1986, as amended) as to a part or a whole of any assets and/or interests of whatever kind or nature that may pass to the undersigned under non-testamentary instruments, under powers of appointment, under testamentary instruments or otherwise. ____ (initials)

2. Make gifts of my assets or any portion or part of them in such amounts and at such times as my Agent deems appropriate to my spouse, if any, and/or one or more of my descendants, including my Agent, however, the amount of any such gift shall not to exceed the annual dollar limits of the federal gift tax exclusion under 26 U.S.C. Section 2503(b), as amended, without regard to whether the federal gift tax exclusion applies to the gift, or if my spouse agrees to consent to a split gift pursuant to 26 U.S.C. Section 2513, as amended, in an amount, per donee, not to exceed twice the annual federal gift tax exclusion limit. My Agent may also consent, pursuant to 26 U.S.C. s. 2513, as amended, to the splitting of a gift made by my spouse, if any, in an amount per donee not to exceed the aggregate annual gift tax exclusions for both spouses. My Agent may make such gifts outright, to a custodian under the Uniform Gifts to Minors Act or the Uniform Transfers to Minors Act, as additions to existing

Exhibit VIII

trusts, or otherwise, as my Agent determines. My Agent is authorized to pay from my assets expenses for medical care and tuition expenses for any of my descendants, including my Agent. Such expenses shall be paid directly to such medical or educational institution. All of my assets shall be available for payment of such expenses. My Agent shall not exercise any authorization granted in this Paragraph 2 in discharge of any legal obligation of such Agent. _____ (initials)

3. Create and fund an inter vivos trust, revocable or irrevocable, as may be necessary to preserve my estate plan, to the extent my estate plan is actually known by my Agent. _____ (initials)

4. With respect to a trust created by or on my behalf, amend, modify, revoke, or terminate the trust as may be necessary to preserve my estate plan, to the extent my estate plan is actually known by my Agent, but only if the trust instrument explicitly provides for amendment, modification, revocation, or termination by my Agent. _____ (initials)

5. Create or change rights of survivorship as may be necessary to preserve my estate plan, to the extent my estate plan is actually known by my Agent. _____ (initials)

6. Create or change a beneficiary designation as may be necessary to preserve my estate plan, to the extent my estate plan is actually known by my Agent. _____ (initials)

7. Waive my right to be a beneficiary of a joint and survivor annuity, including a survivor benefit under a retirement plan as may be necessary to preserve my estate plan, to the extent my estate plan is actually known by my Agent. _____ (initials)

Powers Not Granted to My Agent. Notwithstanding the provisions of this section, an Agent may not:

1. Perform duties under a contract that requires the exercise of my own personal services;

2. Make any affidavit as to my personal knowledge;

3. Vote in any public election on my behalf;

4. Execute or revoke any will or codicil on my behalf; or

5. Exercise powers and authority granted to me as trustee or as court-appointed fiduciary.

Termination of Agent's Authority. My Agent's authority hereunder shall terminate upon the occurrence of any of the events specified in Section 709.2109(2) Florida Statutes Annotated.

Resignation. My Agent may resign by giving written notice to me, any court-appointed guardian, and any co-Agent, or if none, to the next successor Agent.

Compensation. My Agent shall be entitled to reimbursement of expenses reasonably incurred on my behalf. If my Agent is a "qualified agent" within the meaning of 709.2112(4), my Agent

Exhibit VIII

shall be entitled to compensation that is reasonable under the circumstances.

Liability of Agent. My Agent shall not be liable for any act or decision made by such Agent in good faith and under the terms of this Durable Power of Attorney.

Reliance by Third Parties. Any third party who in good faith accepts this Durable Power of Attorney may rely upon the Durable Power of Attorney and the actions of my Agent which are reasonably within the scope of my Agent's authority and may enforce any obligation created by the actions of my Agent as if:

1. The power of attorney were genuine, valid, and still in effect;

2. The Agent's authority were genuine, valid, and still in effect; and

3. The authority of the officer executing for or on behalf of a financial institution that has trust powers and acting as Agent is genuine, valid, and still in effect.

For purposes of this Paragraph, and without limiting what constitutes good faith, a third party does not accept a power of attorney in good faith if the third party has notice that:

1. The power of attorney is void, invalid, or terminated; or

2. The purported Agent's authority is void, invalid, suspended, or terminated.

Liability of Third Parties. Third persons who act in reliance upon the authority granted to my Agent and in accordance with the instructions of my Agent shall be held harmless by the principal from any loss suffered or liability incurred as a result of actions taken before the receipt of notice as provided in Section 709.2121, Florida Statutes Annotated. A third person who acts in good faith upon any representation, direction, decision, or act of my Agent is not liable to the principal or the principal's estate, beneficiaries, or joint owners for those acts.

Noncompliance by Third Parties. If any third party refuses to comply with the provisions of this power, my Agent shall, in an appropriate case, institute an action against such party, seeking recovery of any losses, injunctive relief, punitive damages, and any other relief which my Agent deems appropriate.

Damages; Costs. In any judicial action hereunder, including, but not limited to, the unreasonable refusal of a third party to allow my Agent to act pursuant to the power, and challenges to the proper exercise of authority by my Agent, the prevailing party shall be entitled to damages and costs, including attorney's fees.

Copies. For all purposes, a photocopy or electronically transmitted copy of this Power of Attorney shall have the same effect as the original Power fo Attorney.

Governing Law. This Instrument is executed by me in the State of Florida, which is my State of Domicile, and the laws of

Exhibit VIII

such State shall govern the interpretation of this Instrument. It is my intention that this Power of Attorney shall be exercisable in any other state or jurisdiction where I may own any property or have any interest in property.

Limitation on Appointment of Agent. The appointment of the Agent(s) herein is not a guarantee to such Agent(s) of the right to serve as such. The conduct of the Agent(s) is always subject to judicial review and, in some cases, may lead to disqualification by a Court of Law. Factors which may cause the Agent(s) to fail to qualify for appointment or be removed from his or her representative capacity include, but are not limited to, fitness to serve, disloyalty, bad behavior, and holding or acquiring an adverse interest or an unauthorized conflict of interest.

Signed on _____, 20___.

SAMPLE

TOM TAXPAYER

We certify that the above Instrument was, on the date thereof, signed, sealed, published and declared by TOM TAXPAYER in our presence, and that we, at his request and in his presence, and in the presence of each other, have signed our names as witnesses thereto, believing TOM TAXPAYER to be of sound mind and memory at the time of signing and not under duress or constraint at any time.

_____   _____

Witness/Printed Name   Address

_____   _____

Witness/Printed Name   Address

SWORN TO and subscribed before me this ____ day of _____, 20___.

(SEAL)   _____
                                 Notary Public
                                 State of Florida
                                 My commission expires:

Exhibit VIII

HEALTH CARE SURROGATE DESIGNATION
(POWER OF ATTORNEY)

In the event that I, TOM TAXPAYER, have been determined to be incapacitated to provide informed consent for medical treatment and surgical and diagnostic procedures, I wish to designate as my surrogate for health care decisions:

Name	Address	Telephone

I fully understand that this Designation will permit my Designee to make health care decisions and to provide, withhold or withdraw consent on my behalf; to apply for public benefits to defray the cost of health care; and to authorize my admission to or transfer from a health care facility.

Without limiting the broad powers conferred by the preceding provisions, I authorize my Health Care Surrogate as my Attorney-in-Fact to make any and all health care decisions on my behalf, including, but not limited to, the authority to:

A. Hire and fire medical personnel;

B. Exercise my right of privacy;

C. Consent or withhold consent to both conventional and unconventional medical treatment;

D. Consent or withhold consent to both conventional and unconventional pain relief, drugs or programs;

E. Change accommodations (including, but not limited to changing of hospital, nursing home, or hospice care);

F. Release from liability health care providers for relying on this Power of Attorney and authority of any agent appointed herein; and

G. Review all confidential and other medical and related records and information. I intend for my Surrogate to be treated as I would be with respect to my rights regarding the use and disclosure of my individually identifiable health information or other medical records. This release authorization applies to any information governed by the Health Insurance Portability and Accountability Act of 1996 (a/k/a HIPAA), 42 USC 130 2d and 45 CFR 160-164. I authorize any physician, health care professional, dentist, health plan, hospital, clinic, laboratory, pharmacy or other covered health-care provider, any insurance company and the Medical Information Bureau, Inc. or other health-care clearinghouse that has provided treatment or services to me, or that has paid for or is seeking payment from me for such services, to give, disclose and release to my Surrogate, without

Exhibit IX

restriction, all of my individually identifiable health information and medical records regarding any past, present or future medical or mental health condition, including all information relating to the diagnosis and treatment of HIV/AIDS, sexually transmitted diseases, mental illness, and drug or alcohol abuse. The authority given my agent shall supersede any prior agreement that I may have made with my health-care providers to restrict access to or disclosure of my individually identifiable health information. The authority given my agent has no expiration date and shall expire only in the event that I revoke the authority in writing and deliver it to my health-care provider.

This provision is intended to be a full Durable Power of Attorney for health care decisions and is intended to grant to my Attorney-in-Fact appointed herein all powers described herein, including, but not be limited to all powers provided and authorized under the Life-Prolonging Procedures Act of Florida (Florida Statutes Annotated Section 765.301) and the Florida Medical Consent Law (Florida Statutes Annotated Section 766.103).

This Designation shall not be affected by any physical or mental disability that I may suffer except as provided by statute, and shall be exercisable from this date. All acts done by my Health Care Surrogate pursuant to this Power shall bind me, my heirs, devisees and the Personal Representative(s) of my estate. This Designation shall be and is non-delegable.

This Instrument is governed by the laws of the State of Florida, which is my State of Domicile, but it is my intention that this Designation and Power of Attorney shall be exercisable in any other state or jurisdiction where I may be residing or may be receiving medical treatment.

I hereby confirm all acts of my Health Care Surrogate pursuant to this Power of Attorney, and release and hold harmless all third persons dealing with my Health Care Surrogate who is purporting to act in such capacity under a power or grant of authority contained herein, from such liability, loss or expense as may be incurred by me in connection with actions taken by my Health Care Surrogate Attorney-in-Fact pursuant to this Designation.

Any act that is done under this Designation between the revocation of this Instrument and notice of that revocation to my Health Care Surrogate shall be valid unless the person claiming the benefit of the act had actual notice of that revocation.

The appointment of the Health Care Surrogate(s) and/or Attorney(s)-in-Fact herein is not a guarantee to such Health Care Surrogate(s) and/or Attorney(s)-in-Fact of the right to serve in such capacity. The conduct of the Health Care Surrogate(s) and/or Attorney(s)-in-Fact is always subject to judicial review and, in some cases, may lead to disqualification by a Court of

Exhibit IX

Law. Factors which may cause the Health Care Surrogate(s) and/or Attorney(s)-in-Fact to fail to qualify for appointment or be removed from his or her representative capacity include, but are not limited to, fitness to serve, disloyalty, bad behavior, and holding or acquiring an adverse interest or an unauthorized conflict of interest.

I affirm that this Designation is not being made as a condition to treatment or admission to a health care facility.

Signed, Sealed and Delivered
in the presence of:

SAMPLE

_____   _____
                                         TOM TAXPAYER

_____

SWORN TO and subscribed before me this _____ day of _____, 20___.

(SEAL)   _____
                                Notary Public
                                State of Florida
                                My commission expires:

Exhibit IX

LIVING WILL

By this Declaration, made this _____ day of _____, 20___, I, TOM TAXPAYER, willfully and voluntarily make known my desire that my dying not be artificially prolonged under the circumstances set forth below, and I do hereby declare that, if at any time I am incapacitated and
_____ (initial) I have a terminal condition; or
_____ (initial) I have an end-stage condition; or
_____ (initial) I am in a persistent vegetative state;
and if my attending or treating physician and another consulting physician have determined that there is no medical probability of my recovery from such condition, I direct that life-prolonging procedures be withheld or withdrawn when the application of such procedures would serve only to prolong artificially the process of dying, and that I be permitted to die naturally with only the administration of medication or the performance of any medical procedure deemed necessary to provide me with comfort care or to alleviate pain.

It is my intention that this Declaration be honored by my family and physician as the final expression of my legal right to refuse medical or surgical treatment and to accept the consequences for such refusal.

In the event that I have been determined to be unable to provide express and informed consent regarding the withholding, withdrawal or continuation of life-prolonging procedures, I wish to designate, as my surrogate to carry out the provisions of this Declaration:

Name	Address	Telephone

The appointment of the surrogate(s) herein is not a guarantee to such surrogate(s) of the right to serve in such capacity. The conduct of the surrogate(s) is always subject to judicial review and, in some cases, may lead to disqualification by a Court of Law. Factors which may cause the surrogate(s) to fail to qualify for appointment or be removed from his or her representative capacity include, but are not limited to, fitness to serve, disloyalty, bad behavior, and holding or acquiring an adverse interest or an unauthorized conflict of interest.

I understand the full import of this Declaration, and I am emotionally and mentally competent to make this Declaration.

Exhibit X

Signed, Sealed and Delivered
in the presence of:

SAMPLE

_____

TOM TAXPAYER

_____

SWORN TO and subscribed before me this _____ day of
_____, 20___.

(SEAL)

_____
Notary Public
State of Florida
My commission expires:

Exhibit X

765.101 Definitions - As used in this chapter:

(4) "End-stage condition" means an irreversible condition that is caused by injury, disease, or illness which has resulted in progressively severe and permanent deterioration, and which, to a reasonable degree of medical probability, treatment of the condition would be ineffective.

(12)   "Persistent vegetative state" means a permanent and irreversible condition of unconsciousness in which there is:
    (a) The absence of voluntary action or cognitive behavior of any kind.
    (b) An inability to communicate or interact purposefully with the environment.

(17)   "Terminal condition" means a condition caused by injury, disease, or illness from which there is no reasonable medical probability of recovery and which, without treatment, can be expected to cause death.

Exhibit X

DECLARATION NAMING PRE-NEED GUARDIAN
(Pursuant to Chapter 744.3045, Florida Statutes Annotated)

I, TOM TAXPAYER, presently domiciled and residing at 1 Sunshine Way, City of Paradise, Palm Beach County, Florida, hereby make the following Declaration Naming Pre-Need Guardian to serve in the event of my future incapacity:

If I am at any time determined to be an incapacitated person, as that term is defined in the Florida Guardianship Law as it now exists or may hereafter be amended, I hereby declare that the following individual:

Name	Address	Telephone

is to serve as Plenary Guardian(s) of the Property, to exercise all delegable, legal rights and powers, and to perform all tasks necessary to care for my Property or Estate.

I further declare that the following individual:

Name	Address	Telephone

is to serve as Plenary Guardian(s) of the Person, to exercise all delegable legal rights and powers, and to perform all acts necessary to care for my person.

I further declare that it is my intent and desire that the above-named person(s) be appointed by the Court having jurisdiction to serve in their respective capacities, without bond. Notwithstanding anything to the contrary contained herein, the undersigned hereby acknowledges that the declaration/preference of the Pre-Need Guardian(s) set forth herein is expressly subject to appointment/confirmation of the Designee(s) as Guardian by a Court of competent jurisdiction under Section 744.3045(4/7), Florida Statutes Annotated, as the same now exists or may hereafter be amended, and such declaration herein is **not** a guarantee of appointment as such by any Court of Law. Other

Exhibit XI

considerations and/or qualifications may be considered by a Court of competent jurisdiction, including, but not limited to, issues concerning fitness to serve and/or bad behavior on the part of the Designee(s), which may disqualify the Designee(s) from being entitled to serve in any representative capacity hereunder. See also *Davis v. King*, 686 So.2d 763 (Fla. 5th DCA 1997).

Signed on _____, 20___ .

SAMPLE
_____
TOM TAXPAYER

We certify that the above Instrument was, on the date thereof, signed, sealed, published and declared by TOM TAXPAYER in our presence, and that we, at his request and in his presence, and in the presence of each other, have signed our names as witnesses thereto, believing TOM TAXPAYER to be of sound mind and memory at the time of signing and not under duress or constraint at any time.

_____   _____
Witness/Printed Name   Address

_____   _____
Witness/Printed Name   Address

SWORN TO and subscribed before me this _____ day of _____, 20___ .

(SEAL)   _____
                                                   Notary Public
                                                   State of Florida
                                                   My commission expires:

Exhibit XI

DECLARATION NAMING PRE-NEED GUARDIAN FOR MINOR
(Pursuant to Chapter 744.3046, Florida Statutes Annotated)

I, TOM TAXPAYER, presently domiciled and residing in the City of Paradise, Palm Beach County, Florida, hereby make the following Declaration Naming Pre-Need Guardian for Minor for my minor child, _____, to serve in the event of the adjudication of my incapacity or my death:

I declare that the following individual:

Name	Address	Telephone

is to serve as Guardian(s) of the Person and Property for such minor child.

Signed on _____, 20___.

SAMPLE
_____
TOM TAXPAYER

Exhibit XII

We certify that the above Instrument was, on the date thereof, signed, sealed, published and declared by TOM TAXPAYER in our presence, and that we, at his request and in his presence, and in the presence of each other, have signed our names as witnesses thereto, believing TOM TAXPAYER to be of sound mind and memory at the time of signing and not under duress or constraint at any time.

_____   _____

Witness/Printed Name   Address

_____   _____

Witness/Printed Name   Address

SWORN TO and subscribed before me this ____ day of _____, 20___.

(SEAL)   _____

                                Notary Public
                                State of Florida
                                My commission expires:

Exhibit XII